CONSERVATION SUCCESS

Protecting Wild Spaces and Species

With Hands-On Science Activities for Kids

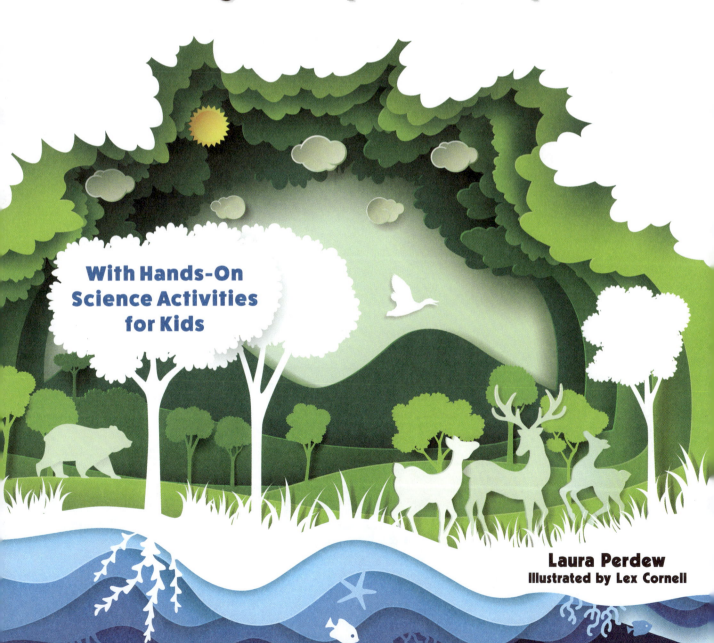

Laura Perdew
Illustrated by Lex Cornell

More science titles from Nomad Press

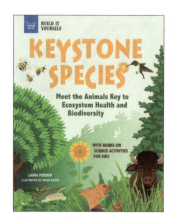
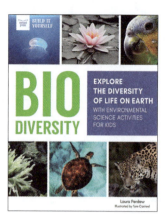
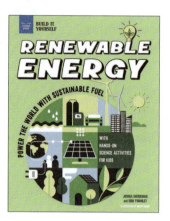
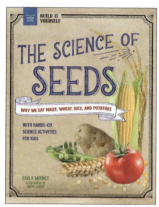

Check out more titles at www.nomadpress.net

Nomad Press

A division of Nomad Communications

10 9 8 7 6 5 4 3 2 1

This book was manufactured by Versa Press, East Peoria, Illinois
May 2025, Job #Q24-67351
ISBN Softcover: 978-1-64741-139-8
ISBN Hardcover: 978-1-64741-136-7

Educational Consultant, Marla Conn

Questions regarding the ordering of this book should be addressed to
Nomad Press
PO Box 1036, Norwich, VT 05055
www.nomadpress.net

Printed in the United States.

CONTENTS

Interested in primary sources? Look for this icon.

Some of the QR codes in this book link to primary sources that offer firsthand information about the topic. Photos are often considered primary sources because a photograph takes a picture at the moment something happens—but watch out for fake ones! Use a smartphone or tablet app to scan the QR code and explore more. You can find a list of the URLs on the Resources page. You can also use the suggested keywords to find other helpful sources.

🔎 conservation

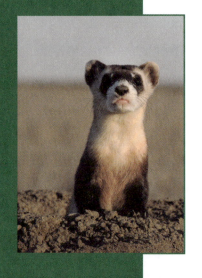

Pre-industrialization: Indigenous peoples steward lands around the world and live in harmony with nature.

Mid-1700s: The Industrial Revolution begins, and the production of goods shifts to factories and greatly increases human impact on the environment.

Late 1700s: Bogd Khan in Mongolia is set aside as a protected area, one of the first national parks in the world.

1872: The first national park in the United States, Yellowstone National Park, is established.

1900: One of the first conservation laws in the United States, the Lacey Act, is enacted to protect wildlife and plants from illegal poaching and trade.

1938: The Hawk Mountain Sanctuary in Pennsylvania is established by Rosalie Edge to protect birds of prey.

1950s: The idea for wildlife bridges originates in France.

1962: American biologist Rachel Carson publishes *Silent Spring*, exposing the dangers of pesticides and raising public awareness.

1972: The United States passes a law banning the use of the pesticide DDT as a direct result of Carson's research.

1973: The Endangered Species Act is signed into law in the United States to protect threatened and endangered species and recover declining populations.

1983: The first large blue butterfly caterpillars are reintroduced in the United Kingdom.

Late 1900s: The concept of rewilding emerges, based on the three Cs: cores, corridors, and carnivores.

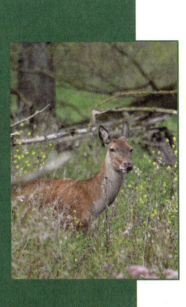

1998: The Khonoma Nature Conservation and Tragopan Sanctuary (KNCTS) in India is established to protect wildlife.

1999: The first five Canada lynx are reintroduced in Colorado after two decades of being extinct in the state.

Early 2000s: The Nepali government envisions a plan to reconnect habitats to protect tigers. In partnership with India and the World Wildlife Fund, the Terai Arc Landscape in Asia now spans nearly 20,000 square miles.

2004: The reintroduction of the Eurasian beaver project begins in Serbia.

2006: Panamanian biologist Edgardo Griffith opens a frog hotel to save the critically endangered Panamanian golden frog and other amphibians.

2008: The Gregg Carr Foundation enters into a partnership with the government of Mozambique to rehabilitate Gorongosa National Park.

2012–2013: The Penobscot Nation removes three dams on the Penobscot River in Maine, reopening passage for migrating fish.

2014: The city of Oslo, Norway, initiates a plan for a bee highway to support bees and other insects.

2019: Costa Rica earns the United Nations' top environmental honor, the Champion of the Earth Award.

2022: Eighty-two Native tribes manage 20,000 bison in the United States.

2023: Kākāpō in New Zealand number more than 200 after decades of work to recover the bird's population.

2024: The number of tigers in the Terai Arc Landscape in Asia is double what it was when the project began two decades earlier.

CONSERVATION
IN ACTION

Imagine a thriving **wetland** where a trash dump used to be. Birds come and go. Frogs chirp and croak among the green plants. Turtles bask on logs. The clean, clear water trickles softly.

Now, picture a Canada lynx prowling the mountains of Colorado after being gone from the state for decades. She moves silently through the snow, stalking her **prey**. She mates with another lynx that was reintroduced and will give birth to a new litter in the spring.

ESSENTIAL QUESTION

Why is conservation so important?

Take a moment to visualize a **wildlife corridor** over a busy highway. The cars and trucks rush by below, while up above, **wildlife** crosses safely. Their **habitats** are again connected. These are not made-up stories, but true accounts that reveal the power of **conservation**.

In the news, we often hear the worst stories about what is happening to our planet, the **environment**, **natural resources**, and wild **species**. These problems seem so big and they can be overwhelming. Frightening stories often overshadow amazing, ongoing conservation efforts happening all over the world, on every continent and in every type of habitat. Countless conservation projects have already been successful. People are making a difference.

THE HISTORY OF CONSERVATION

What is conservation? Conservation is the purposeful act of taking care of the natural world. It's the recovery of habitats and the protection of **biodiversity**. It's about looking toward the future. However, as you will learn in this book, conservation is much more than that!

Conservation looks different in different places. Sometimes, conservation is simple, such as picking up trash in a natural area. Some conservation efforts are very complex and require science and **technology** to help people make decisions about how to help.

This wildlife corridor in Poland allows animals to safely move from one area to another.

We didn't always need conservation. For thousands and thousands of years, **indigenous** peoples have lived in **harmony** with nature, connected to the land. But as the human population grew, others started to think differently about nature. Instead of living in harmony with nature, they wanted to control it. They wanted to tame it.

However, as early as the mid-1600s, people began to notice the impact they were having on the natural world. For example, in England, a man named John Evelyn (1620–1706) called attention to **deforestation**. His writings highlighted the need to preserve forests and reestablish new trees. He was one of the first conservationists.

WORDS TO KNOW

Industrial Revolution: a period during the eighteenth and nineteenth centuries when large-scale production of goods began and large cities and factories began to replace small towns and farming.

rural: in the countryside, as opposed to a city.

urban: in a city or large town.

agrarian: relating to farmed land.

industrialized: having many businesses and factories involved in producing goods.

geologist: a scientist who studies geology, which is the history and structure of the earth and its rocks.

geologic timescale: the way time is divided into large blocks to describe the 4.6-billion-year history of the earth.

Anthropocene: a geologic time during which humans have had a great impact on Earth's environment and climate.

over-exploitation: the taking of a natural resource faster than it can reproduce or be replenished. To exploit means to use something for personal gain without respect for the consequences.

invasive species: a plant or animal that is not native to an area and may cause it harm.

climate change: the long-term change in temperature and weather patterns across a large area, in particular attributed to the use of fossil fuels as an energy source.

Others followed, especially in the mid-1700s during the **Industrial Revolution**. This was when many people moved from **rural** to **urban** areas. Societies that were once **agrarian** became **industrialized**. Goods were produced in factories instead of being made by hand. People lived in cities instead of on farms. Transportation improved.

One of the first protected areas in the world is in Mongolia. The Bogd Khan Uul Strictly Protected Area was established during the eighteenth century, though there is evidence of informal protection dating back to the 1100s.

The Scientific Method

A scientific method worksheet is a useful tool for keeping your ideas and observations organized. The scientific method is the process scientists use to ask and answer questions. Use a notebook as a science journal to make a scientific method worksheet for each experiment you do.

Question: What are we trying to find out? What problem are we trying to solve?
Research: What is already known about this topic?
Hypothesis: What do we think the answer will be?
Equipment: What supplies are we using?
Method: What procedure are we following?
Results: What happened and why?

More and more land was taken for cities, roads, businesses, and homes as well as for agriculture to feed growing populations. Wild animals that were seen as a threat were killed. Humans had an even greater impact on the environment.

> **Meet a conservation biologist in this video.** Learn about the work a conservation biologist does and how to become one. What are different ways individuals who aren't scientists can become part of wildlife conservation?
>
> 🔍 Camp TV conservation biologist

Even as people were harming the natural world around them, they had a renewed appreciation for nature. People had more free time for outdoor activities. Those living in urban areas began to take trips into the wilderness to escape the crowded cities. Advances in transportation made travel to wild spaces easier.

As this new appreciation for nature developed, people began to recognize that natural resources were being used up and wild species were disappearing. The roots of the modern conservation movement took hold in the 1800s.

Welcome to the Anthropocene

Geologists have created a calendar of Earth's events through time. Each part of the **geologic timescale** has a different name. The modern geologic time is often called the **Anthropocene**, though it has not been officially labeled by geologists. The word *Anthropocene* means "the age of man." Why? Because humans have had such a deep impact on the planet.

Although this book is about conservation, it is important to know why we need conservation in the first place. The impacts that people first noticed in the 1600s have continued to this day. Human activity has resulted in habitat loss, **over-exploitation** of natural resources, the introduction of **invasive species**, **climate change**, and the pollution of land, water, and air. Each of these has had widespread consequences, giving rise to dedicated conservationists fighting to protect nature and the environment.

> To learn more about the Anthropocene, listen to the podcast *Landscapes of the Anthropocene*. What is the evidence that we are living in the Anthropocene?
>
>
>
> 🔍 Anthropocene for Kids

CONSERVATION SUCCESS

Conservation organizations emerged, including the Audubon Society, whose members wanted to protect birds. Yellowstone National Park, the first national park in the United States, was established in 1872. Writers, artists, and photographers of the time focused much of their work on natural landscapes of the West. Their art raised awareness about the need to protect those areas from development.

Theodore Roosevelt is often referred to as the "conservationist president."

President Theodore Roosevelt (1858–1919) also played a key role in the conservation movement. He established nature reserves and created five national parks. Plus, he stood up to people who wanted to harm the environment for personal **profit**.

Young Conservationist: Licypriya Kangujam (India)

Licypriya Kangujam (2011–) started her career as an environmental activist at age six in her home in India. She fights climate change and pollution in order to protect the environment. "Asking [for] clean air to breathe, clean water to drink, and a clean planet to live [on] are our basic rights. I'm a child who strongly believes that children can lead the change." Kangujam has brought this message before world leaders at the United Nations Climate Change Conference. She's given several TEDx talks and led marches and protests. She is a leader and inspiration to kids around the world calling for action to fight climate change.

Learn more about Kangujam and her work, awards, and foundation on her website. Why do you think she has become such an inspiration for young people?

🔎 Who is Licypriya Kangujam

PRESERVATION OR CONSERVATION?

As people grew more aware about their relationship with nature, they debated what to do to protect the natural world. That debate continues today. Some people want to set aside land so that it stays completely free of human impact. **Preservationists** want the land to be completely protected from use—no roads, no camping, no logging, no hunting, and no human use other than by indigenous peoples.

Conservationists, on the other hand, still want to use natural resources and wild places, but they want this use to be regulated and limited. Their goal is **sustainability**. They support the wise use of natural resources now *and* protection of nature for the future. That might allow for some roads, hiking trails, and maybe even a campground after careful planning. Use would be regulated and monitored. For example, if hunting and fishing were allowed, people would need a permit, and the number of permits issued would be limited.

The focus of this book is conservation.

The Great Backyard Bird count enlists the help of hundreds of thousands of citizen science volunteers every year. The data collected helps scientists monitor and protect birds around the world.

Theodore Roosevelt and environmentalist John Muir on Glacier Point, Yosemite Valley, California, in 1903

Credit: Underwood & Underwood

CONSERVATION SUCCESS

WORDS TO KNOW

restoration: the recovery of a damaged or destroyed habitat to its natural state.

rewilding: the restoration of an ecosystem and its biodiversity to minimize human impact and let nature take care of itself.

reintroduction: the process of returning a species to an area where it once lived but had been absent from.

reconnecting: the reestablishment of a connection between two habitats.

ecosystem: an interdependent community of living and nonliving things and their environment.

ecotourism: tourism that responsibly protects wildlife and the environment and supports conservation.

culture: the beliefs and way of life of a group of people, which can include religion, language, art, clothing, food, and holidays.

prairie: a vast area of open grassland.

holistic: considering the whole of something, not just its parts.

TYPES OF CONSERVATION EFFORTS

Think back to our earlier vision of the thriving wetland that used to be a dump. That thriving habitat is the result of **restoration**. Do you notice the connection to the word "restore"?

Other conservation efforts include **rewilding**, **reintroduction**, recovering species, and **reconnecting**. Do you detect a pattern in each of these words? They all start with the prefix *re-*, which means "back" or "again." Many conservation efforts work to return **ecosystems** and wildlife to the way they were before human impact.

You can participate in a bird count! Find out how to become a citizen scientist helping to protect the world's birds at the Cornell Lab of Ornithology website. Why might it be important to count birds?

🔎 citizen science bird count

Community-based conservation is led by local people living in the area in need of management and protection. **Ecotourism** is an approach to tourism that minimizes the impact of visitors to a place while raising awareness about the local **culture** and the need for conservation. Of course, protections, laws, and education are also key parts of conservation. This book looks at each type of approach.

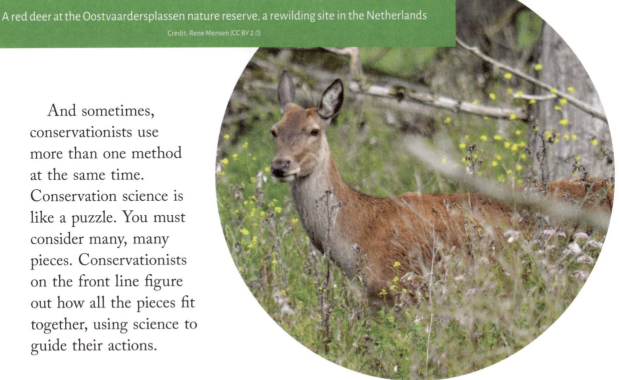

A red deer at the Oostvaardersplassen nature reserve, a rewilding site in the Netherlands
Credit: Rene Mensen (CC BY 2.0)

And sometimes, conservationists use more than one method at the same time. Conservation science is like a puzzle. You must consider many, many pieces. Conservationists on the front line figure out how all the pieces fit together, using science to guide their actions.

Holistic Conservation

In Canada, only 30 percent of the country's original **prairies** remain. The rest have been lost to oil and gas production and agriculture. To protect and heal the prairie ecosystem, Grasslands National Park in Canada has launched a conservation effort with a multi-pronged approach. This includes planting native species of plants such as sagebrush. The government also reintroduced bison to the region and is currently managing those herds. These efforts improve habitats for key species such as sage-grouse and black-tailed prairie dogs. Planned fires help reduce invasive species and promote growth of native ones. In addition, the park educates the public about the importance of the mixed-grass prairie ecosystem. Together, these efforts are a powerful, **holistic** approach to conservation.

WORDS TO KNOW

life cycle: the growth and changes a living thing goes through, from birth to death.

data: facts or pieces of information, often given in the form of numbers, that can be processed by a computer.

organism: something living, such as a plant or an animal.

acoustic monitoring: the use of sound recordings to collect information about different species.

SCIENCE AND TECHNOLOGY

Scientists of all kinds study different species, their needs, and their **life cycles**. They also study habitats and ecosystems to understand how they work. All the information they collect is important and guides the work they do! And science and technology play key roles in their work.

Let's say your bicycle chain breaks. To learn how to fix it, what would you do first? You'd study a bike! You'd learn how the chain works and fits onto the gear. You might also ask for help from an expert. It's the same with conservation. The more knowledge conservationists have about a species or ecosystem and how it works, the more effectively they can help. The knowledge scientists collect not only guides their actions, it also raises awareness.

The more the public knows about and understands conservation, the more likely it is to support it.

Technology can be a huge help in gathering information and carrying out conservation efforts. We use it to collect **data** and monitor species and ecosystems. Scientists fit collars and tracking devices on some **organisms** to track their movements and learn more about the species. Camera traps and drones are also useful monitoring tools. Satellites in space provide information about changes to an ecosystem and its health. Powerful computers analyze data and images.

Essential Questions

Each chapter of this book begins with an essential question to help guide your exploration of conservation. Keep the question in mind as you read the chapter. At the end of each chapter, use your science journal to record your thoughts and answers.

ESSENTIAL QUESTION

Why is conservation so important?

People use bird banding to identify and track birds. This doesn't hurt the birds!

Acoustic monitoring is another example of how scientists use technology in conservation. They place sensors in the field to monitor wildlife for long periods of time. The sound recordings provide scientists with information about the species in an area. This information helps identify changes in species behavior and communication as well as track human impact.

Let's dive in and learn about different conservation efforts happening all around the world!

Listen to whales! Deep in Monterey Bay in California, whales are having long conversations—and you can eavesdrop! How do recordings such as this help scientists study whales?

🔎 Monterey humpback song

PS

TEXT TO WORLD

Do you have any natural areas near where you live? How do they stay undeveloped?

CREATE A
SOUND MAP

Scientists use acoustic monitoring to help them understand the variety of species that live in an area and the human influence on that area. Create a sound map for your neighborhood. You don't need any fancy equipment, just your ears, science journal, and a pencil.

❯ **Find a spot to sit, preferably away from the sounds of roads and other human-made noises.**

❯ **On your paper, draw a large circle with an X in the middle.** The X indicates your location.

❯ **Close your eyes.** What do you hear? Mark what you hear and where you hear it on your map. Your mark can be a symbol or word, whatever works for you. Sounds near to you will be close to your X. Sounds off in the distance will be farther away from your X.

❯ **Listen for two minutes.** Then turn 90 degrees in one direction. Listen for two more minutes. Repeat this four times. While listening, you may want to cup your hands around your ears to help you hear sounds. Natural sounds may come from animals or insects, but you may also hear the sound of wind or water or rustling leaves.

✱ What does your map look like when you're finished?

✱ Are there more sounds in one particular location?

Try This!

Consider doing a sound map at different times on the same day. Are the sounds similar? Are they different? You might even consider doing a sound map at the same time of day once a month. Pay attention to the similarities and differences in the sounds you hear.

Chapter 1

ECOSYSTEM
RESTORATION

Natural ecosystems are complex networks of interdependent parts. When the parts work together, the ecosystem stays healthy and runs smoothly. But when these parts get disturbed, the ecosystem can become unbalanced.

Think about a car engine. All the parts of the engine keep a car running smoothly. But if you take out or interfere with a part, or a part breaks, the car does not run well. It might not work at all. The same happens in an ecosystem.

Unlike a car, nature is good at restoring itself. It can often renew and **regenerate** itself after a disturbance. However, sometimes an ecosystem is so damaged that it needs a little help from humans.

ESSENTIAL QUESTION

What strategies do scientists use to restore ecosystems?

WORDS TO KNOW

regenerate: the ability to renew, reestablish, or recover from damage.

degraded: harmed to the point where an ecosystem does not function properly.

hydrology: the distribution and movement of water in an ecosystem.

nutrient cycle: how nutrients, the substances in food and soil that living things need to grow and survive, move through an ecosystem.

food web: a network of connected food chains that shows the complex set of feeding relationships between plants and animals.

endangered: at risk of becoming extinct.

clear-cutting: to remove every tree from an area.

livestock: animals raised for food and other uses.

crops: plants grown for food and other uses.

fossil fuel: a fuel such as oil, coal, or natural gas, which takes millions of years to form from the remains of plant and animals.

incentive: a reward that encourages someone to do something.

greenhouse gas: a gas in the atmosphere that traps heat. Too much greenhouse gas contributes to global warming.

atmosphere: a layer of gases around the earth.

How do people restore ecosystems? To restore a damaged or **degraded** ecosystem, people actively repair it to bring back its natural functions. Scientists research what needs to be done and work to understand the complex systems within that ecosystem, such as the **hydrology**, **nutrient cycles**, and **food webs** as well as the life cycles of the species that live there. Then, they get to work!

Let's look at some successful restoration projects.

The ecosystems of Costa Rica support about 500,000 different species of plants and animals, including many rare and endangered species.

COSTA RICA

If countries got gold stars for conservation efforts, Costa Rica would get one! In fact, in 2019, the small Central American country did earn the United Nations' top environmental honor, the Champion of the Earth award. Costa Rica is a model to other countries for its use of renewable energy and protection of land, sea, and coral reefs. Costa Rica was also the first tropical country to reverse deforestation.

In 1987, forest covered only 40 percent of Costa Rica. By 2022, forest covered close to 60 percent. Much of the forest restoration was done on the local level, with many people contributing across the country.

This forest restoration was badly needed following decades of **clear-cutting** to make space for raising **livestock** and growing **crops**. First, in 1996, the country enacted a ban on cutting trees without a permit. Then, it established the Payment of Environmental Services (PES) program, which pays landowners to restore their land and protect forests and watersheds. The money comes from a tax on **fossil fuels**. With this financial **incentive** from the government, many landowners have restored their land to dense, productive forest.

The PES program saved more forest from being cut and resulted in 7 million trees being planted. Not only is this conservation effort restoring the forests, it is also protecting and supporting biodiversity. Capuchin monkeys, red-eyed tree frogs, and many other species thrive in the forests. Plus, it's part of the fight against climate change—trees absorb carbon, reducing the amount of this **greenhouse gas** in the **atmosphere**.

La Amistad International Park in Costa Rica

WORDS TO KNOW

erosion: the gradual wearing away of rock or soil by water and wind.

hazardous waste: a waste with properties that make it dangerous or potentially harmful to human health or the environment.

revegetate: to replant and rebuild the soil of disturbed land.

migrate: to move from one environment to another when seasons change.

The PES program is a source of pride to Costa Ricans, and these conservation values will be passed down through generations.

TOXIC WASTELAND TO TEEMING WILDERNESS

Ohio has another example of wilderness restoration. In 1985, the National Park Service (NPS) purchased a piece of property—the Krejci Dump—in Cuyahoga Valley, Ohio. The NPS thought the dump was simply a scrap yard, but when people began cleanup efforts in the mid-1980s, the NPS discovered toxic waste. For decades, a variety of hazardous materials was left at the Krejci Dump. The result was contaminated water and soil. The river was dead and had no fish. The wetland was a wasteland. One ecologist at the park called the area a "biological desert."

Wetlands are called the "kidneys of the planet" because they filter water. They also slow and stop erosion, store water, protect coastlines from storms, and provide habitats for plants and animals.

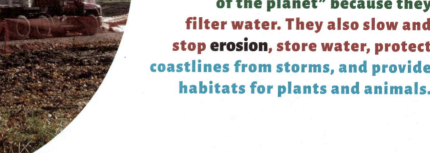

Toxic soil being removed from the Krejci Dump

Citizen Science

Citizen science is a powerful conservation tool. It can take a few scientists years or even decades to collect the data they need to understand and protect certain species or ecosystems. That's where citizen scientists can help! People of all ages, all around the world, can help collect data using smartphones, apps, social media, and other technologies.

For example, Great Smoky Mountains National Park in North Carolina and Tennessee set up the Otter Spotter program. Visitors who see an otter in the park add the sighting to a database. The information allows rangers to monitor the otters that were reintroduced there in 1986. Similarly, visitors to the Grand Canyon in Arizona report sightings of monarch butterflies and the milkweed they depend on. That information is used for the Milkweed Mapper Project, which creates maps of where milkweed grows to help with conservation efforts.

Use the PBS Kids website to find a citizen science project near you! How can your role as a citizen scientist help conservation?

🔎 PBS citizen science

After closing the area to the public, the Environmental Protection Agency (EPA) and the NPS started the cleanup of the 40-acre site. They removed leaking barrels and other solid waste.

Soon it became clear that the problem was much worse and much deeper in the ground than anyone had imagined. To remove all the buried trash, barrels, and polluted soil, the cleanup crews had to dig down 25 feet in some places. In total, they removed 375,000 tons of waste and polluted soil and disposed of them in proper **hazardous waste** sites.

With the waste gone, the land was shaped to match what it once looked like. The wetlands were **revegetated** with native plants. As years passed, the plants thrived. Wildlife returned. Today, if you visit Cuyahoga Valley National Park, you will not see any evidence of the toxic site it once was. Instead, you might see bald eagles, **migrating** waterfowl, salamanders, wildflowers, and much, much more.

WORDS TO KNOW

ecosystem engineer: a species that greatly alters an ecosystem by creating, modifying, maintaining, or destroying it.

drought: a long period of unusually low rainfall that can harm plants and animals.

keystone species: a species that plays a vital role in an ecosystem and without which the ecosystem would be greatly altered.

FREE LABOR

In the Cuyahoga Valley, the ecosystem was entirely recreated—with a lot of money. Do you know what else can restore wetlands? Beavers! And they work for free.

During the 1700s and 1800s in North America, beavers were over-hunted. Without beavers, the river and wetland ecosystems they create with their dams collapsed. Scientists have since discovered the key role beavers play as **ecosystem engineers**. Their dams slow moving water, create habitats for plants and animals, and increase biodiversity. Ponds store water and groundwater is replenished. The ponds filter the water, improving water quality.

Downstream from a beaver dam, water flows more steadily, which reduces flooding and erosion. In addition, beaver ponds provide protection against wildfires and **drought**. Because so many species rely on beavers, they are considered a **keystone species**. Researchers realized that beavers could be essential to restoring degraded river ecosystems.

In Bridge Creek, Oregon, however, the river system was too degraded for the few remaining beavers to restore the ecosystem. Their dams often blew out within a year or two because the water flowed too fast. In 2007, one scientist had a simple and low-tech idea to give the beavers a hand—beaver dam analogues (BDAs) that mimic beaver dams. The Bridge Creek team of scientists installed 121 of these analogues by pounding posts vertically into the stream bed and then weaving sticks and other material around them horizontally to mimic a beaver dam.

As hoped, the BDAs attracted beavers! The beavers even spread throughout the stream system beyond the analogue installations.

For more information on how the work of beavers maintains and restores ecosystems, watch the video on this page. How do beavers help fight climate change?

🔎 Conversation beavers climate

Within a few years, the beavers had reinforced about 60 of the analogue dams. More importantly, they built 115 new dams. The Bridge Creek team saw improvements to the habitat in one to three years, much faster than expected.

As a result of the beavers' river ecosystem restoration, fish and other wildlife returned, too. One study showed that the restored Bridge Creek had close to three times more fish than another degraded stream where BDAs were not installed.

REBUILDING CORAL REEFS

Coral reefs are often called the "**rainforests** of the sea" because they provide food and shelter to so many **marine** species. Like beavers, coral reefs are a keystone species! Although coral reefs cover only 1 percent of the ocean floor, more than 25 percent of all marine species rely on reefs during part of their life cycle.

Young Conservationist: Jadav Payeng (India)

When Jadav Payeng (1959–) was young, he witnessed deforestation near his home in India. The deforestation changed the ecosystem and left Majuli Island and nearby areas subject to flooding and erosion as well as drought. When he was 16, Payeng discovered hundreds of snakes that had died stranded on a sandbar. That scene motived him to act.

In 1979, he started planting one tree sapling a day on Majuli Island near where he had found the snakes. As many decades passed, Payeng continued his mission, planting and tending the saplings. The forest grew and grew to more than 1,300 acres! As the forest grew, so did its biodiversity. Today, the forest is home to hundreds of species of animals. For his work, Payeng earned many awards and honors as well as the title, "The Forest Man of India."

Credit: Medhi jyoti (CC BY SA 4.0)

Listen to this podcast from **National Oceanic and Atmospheric Administration (NOAA) Fisheries** to **learn about the restoration of coral reefs in Florida Keys National Marine Sanctuary.** How are scientists responding to the threats coral face?

🔎 NOAA Fisheries restoring coral

For many reasons, including pollution and climate change, coral reefs are suffering.

Coral reef restoration involves reducing pollution, making corals more resilient in the face of climate change, removing invasive species of **algae**, and enforcing sustainable fishing practices. Another option is direct restoration, which involves raising coral in nurseries.

Researchers discovered that playing the sounds of a healthy coral reef underwater significantly improved the health of coral lava!

Ocean-based coral nurseries consist of manmade, tree-like structures anchored on the ocean floor. Divers collect fragments of coral that have broken off a reef, perhaps from a powerful storm or collision with a boat.

WORDS TO KNOW

predator: an animal that hunts and eats other animals.

spawn: to produce eggs or young.

genetic diversity: the variety of genes within a species.

photomosaic: a large picture created using many small photos.

intertidal: the zone where the ocean meets the land between low and high tides.

subtropical: an area close to the tropics where the weather is warm.

tropical: the hot climate zone to the north and south of the equator.

reptile: an animal such as a snake, lizard, alligator, or turtle that has a spine, lays eggs, has scales or horny places, and breathes air. Reptiles are cold-blooded, so they need sunlight to keep warm and shade to stay cool.

runoff: water that flows off the land into bodies of water. It picks up wastes as it flows over the surface of the ground. Runoff can pollute streams, lakes, rivers, and oceans.

They hang these fragments on the nursery trees, like pieces of laundry. The fragments dangle in the water, safe from **predators**, for about a year.

During this time, scientists and volunteers visit the nursery to check on the progress of the coral. They also remove any algae, which can smother the corals.

Once the coral has grown, scientists transplant it by gluing or tying it to a degraded reef. Gluing bits of coral to a reef does not sound very scientific, but it works! The transplanted corals help degraded reefs recover and add to the diversity of corals on a reef. Scientists know the restoration was successful if the transplanted corals **spawn**, giving life to new generations of coral.

NOAA has many coral nurseries in the Caribbean. Other organizations work to restore coral as well. Much of the coral transplanted in the Caribbean is staghorn and elkhorn coral, which both grow rather quickly. Scientists are still investigating how to best grow other species of coral to increase **genetic diversity**, which is important to an ecosystem's health and strength.

Divers monitor coral reefs and nurseries with underwater cameras and image processing software that can map the reefs using **photomosaics**. This information allows scientists to monitor the health and growth of newly planted corals. Plus, the data is useful for planning future restoration efforts.

Watch this video about the Kissimmee River Restoration in Florida. Why was it important to restore the river to its natural state?

Vimeo Kissimmee restoration

Restoration is an important part of conservation. In the next chapter, we'll look at another technique— rewilding.

ESSENTIAL QUESTION

What strategies do scientists use to restore ecosystems?

The Value of Mangroves

Mangrove forests are coastal wetlands found in **intertidal** zones in **subtropical** and **tropical** areas. Mangroves provide habitats for fish, **reptiles**, birds, and other wildlife. The root systems of mangroves act like anchors and prevent soil and sand erosion. Also, by filtering **runoff**, they protect seagrass beds and coral reefs from toxins. And they help to fight climate change by absorbing and storing carbon.

To restore lost mangrove forests, researcher Robin Lewis (1944–2018) began work in 1986 to identify the perfect conditions for mangrove seedlings to grow—the process is different from planting trees on land. He found that mangrove seedlings are most likely to survive when they are dry 70 percent of the time and submerged by the tide the remaining 30 percent. By creating these conditions at a coastal site, Lewis found that mangroves naturally reestablished themselves. Lewis's method has been used successfully in dozens of projects in the United States and around the world.

OIL SPILL
CLEANUP

As people drill for and transport oil, sometimes there are spills. These spills can occur on land, but more often they happen in the ocean. Oil spills harm marine ecosystems and wildlife. To begin restoring these ecosystems, scientists and engineers have devised ways to clean up the oil. Try this experiment to see how to remove oil from water.

IDEAS FOR SUPPLIES

- tray for water
- vegetable oil
- cotton balls or squares
- sponge
- paper towel
- spoon
- syringe
- science journal
- pencil

❯ **Fill your tray with water, about ½ to 1 inch deep.** Pour a few tablespoons of oil into the water.

❯ **Skim the water's surface with each of the different absorbent materials.**

✱ Which ones remove the oil most effectively?

✱ Do some pick up just the oil, while others pick up both water and oil?

❯ **Try removing the oil with the syringe.** How effective is that compared to the absorbent materials?

❯ **Try building something in the water to contain the oil.** This could be a wall of rocks or perhaps a floating boom around your "oil spill" to keep it from spreading. What works best?

Try This!

Wildlife, including birds, is harmed during oil spills. The oil sticks to the bird's feathers, makes it heavy, and prevents the bird from flying. One of the methods used to help birds and other animals is to give them a gentle bath in Dawn dish soap. This product is known for removing grease and oil from not only dishes but animals, too. Try putting a few drops of Dawn in your tray. What happens? If you have a bird feather, soak it in oil and observe the feather. Wash it with Dawn. How effective is the soap in removing the oil?

RESTORATION
FLIPBOOK

Ecosystem restoration takes time. Whether left alone or helped by humans, nature renews and regenerates slowly. Imagine a time lapse of tropical forest restoration, with the land transforming from barren farmland back to lush forest. Create a flipbook that illustrates this process.

IDEAS FOR SUPPLIES

- 10 to 20 pieces of paper, about 2 x 3 inches, or a stack of sticky notes
- art supplies
- science journal
- pencil

> **Research tropical forest biodiversity and how this ecosystem might transform from farm to forest.**

> **Plan what will go on each piece of paper.** How will the rainforest recover a little bit from page to page? Consider what new trees or plants might grow, how they might get taller or denser, and what new animals might appear.

> **Stack your pieces of paper and secure them on the left edge with tape or staples.**

> **Start drawing, beginning on the last page of the flipbook.** Make small changes on each page as you move forward in the book so that when flipped, there will appear to be movement or growth. Add your name and a title to the front cover.

Check out this web page for additional instructions and a video about how to make a flipbook.

🔍 Kansas discovery flipbook

Try This!

Take what you learned about tropical rainforest restoration and turn it into a stop-motion video! You can use the pictures you drew for your flipbook or you could gather toys and other items to create a 3-D video. Share your creation with friends and family.

TEXT TO **WORLD**

What might your neighborhood look like if it was restored to a time 10 years earlier? What about 500 years earlier?

Chapter 2

READY FOR
REWILDING

The goals of restoration and rewilding are the same—to recover an ecosystem. Sometimes, rewilding can be part of restoration and vice versa. So, what's the difference between the two methods? Good question! While restoration tends to consist of hands-on projects to repair an ecosystem, rewilding is more hands-off—nature is left to heal itself. But humans still need to pay attention and monitor the area being rewilded.

ESSENTIAL QUESTION

How is rewilding an effective approach to conservation?

The concept of rewilding emerged during the late 1900s based on the three Cs: cores, corridors, and **carnivores**. The strategies based on the three Cs include preserving core wilderness areas, creating wildlife corridors to keep wilderness areas connected, and bringing in carnivores to help rebuild food webs.

We'll look at how these three strategies work together to rewild ecosystems, and we'll take an even closer look at wildlife corridors in Chapter 5.

More recently, these strategies have expanded to include bringing in other animals—not just carnivores—and plants, too. The emphasis is on increasing biodiversity so that an ecosystem recovers its natural functions. Nature reestablishes itself and becomes self-sustaining with minimal human management. This type of conservation has no specific end goal or timeline. Nature is allowed to do what nature does best—regenerate itself.

Watch this video from TedEd to learn more about the role biodiversity plays in ecosystems. Why is biodiversity important to an ecosystem?

🔎 TedEd biodiversity Preshoff

Let's look at some rewilding projects that demonstrate the benefits of giving the land back to the wildlife and the wildlife back to the land.

THE KNEPP ESTATE

"In wildness is the preservation of the world."

—Henry David Thoreau, American environmentalist and essayist (1817–1862)

In 1983, Charlie Burrell (1962–) inherited a castle in West Sussex, England. The Knepp Castle had been in his family for more than 200 years and Charlie Burrell was its 10th owner. He inherited the castle plus a 3,500-acre estate with a farm on it. He and his wife, Isabella Tree, tried to continue farming the land, but nothing grew well in the clay soil. After they struggled for many years and invested a lot of money, they admitted defeat.

Then, the couple learned about rewilding from Dutch ecologist Frans Vera (1949–). After a conversation with Vera in the early 2000s, Burrell and Tree decided to give the land back to nature.

WORDS TO KNOW

herbivore: an animal that eats only plants.

aerate: to allow air to flow through.

feces: poop.

pollinate: to transfer pollen from the male parts of flowers to the female parts so that flowers can make seeds.

decompose: to rot or break down.

organic: something that is or was living, such as animals, wood, grass, and insects. Also refers to food grown naturally, without chemicals.

nutrients: substances in food, water, and soil that living things need to live and grow.

depleted: used up.

satellite remote sensing: the use of special cameras to monitor an area's physical characteristics from a distance.

They still owned the land, but they stopped farming and managing it. They removed fences and restored the natural hydrology by removing drainage ditches and allowing water to run the way it used to.

They also brought to the land a few different **herbivores** such as an ancient breed of English longhorn cattle, pigs, and horses. Why? Because these grazing animals used to play key roles in the ecosystem.

Through the way they feed and move around, grazers **aerate** the soil with their hooves. They graze on grasses and trees, acting like natural pruners. They transport seeds across an area on their fur and hooves and in their **feces**. That poop also fertilizes the soil. By bringing back the herbivores, the owners of the castle hoped these native animals would give nature a jump start.

Insects

Insects are an important part of rewilding. Although often overlooked or viewed as pests, insects are key to ecosystem health. As American biologist E.O. Wilson (1929-2021) said, "If all mankind were to disappear, the world would regenerate back to the rich state of equilibrium that existed ten thousand years ago. If insects were to vanish, the environment would collapse into chaos."

Insects **pollinate** plants, which is essential to plant reproduction. They also play a valuable role in **decomposing** decaying **organic** materials and recycling **nutrients**. And they're a food source for a variety of other wildlife! The services provided by insects support and promote the biodiversity of plants and animals in an ecosystem. That biodiversity, in turn, creates a stronger, healthier ecosystem.

Nature returned quickly. Birds, bats, snakes, countless insect species, and other wildlife, including many that are endangered or rare, found their way to Knepp. Knepp is now also home to a variety of plants, grasses, and trees, all on land that was once completely **depleted**.

The Knepp Estate was home to a breeding pair of white storks. It was the first time white storks had bred successfully in Britain in more than 600 years.

The rewilding of the Knepp Estate was monitored by **satellite remote sensing** so scientists could study the effectiveness of rewilding as a conservation approach. Across two decades, the scientists used data and images provided by satellites to watch the recovery of the estate. The long-term monitoring clearly revealed the success of rewilding at Knepp. In addition, it provided insights into the best time to introduce animals to different areas. All this monitoring data is very useful for planning future rewilding projects.

Knepp serves as an inspiration and role model for rewilding projects as well as a research hub for scientists and conservationists. Not only that, Knepp is now generating more money than it did when it was a farm. People visit Knepp for research and ecotourism. We will discuss ecotourism in detail in Chapter 7.

Longhorn cattle free ranging at Knepp Wildland
Credit: PeterEastern (CC BY-SA 4.0)

GORONGOSA NATIONAL PARK

When Gorongosa National Park in Mozambique was established in 1960, it was home to zebras, lions, elephants, hippos, wildebeest, and many more species of African wildlife. But in 1977, civil war broke out and the park lost 95 percent of its wildlife, which was killed for money or food. Even after the war ended in 1992, **poachers** were still active in the area.

Enter Gregg Carr (1959–), a successful entrepreneur turned activist and **philanthropist**. In 2004, he met Mozambique's then president, Joaquim Chissano (1939–), who asked for help in rehabilitating the national park. Carr agreed and, starting in 2008, the Greg Carr Foundation began a 20-year contract with Mozambique's government.

Drones are used to create maps of conservation sites and monitor ecosystem recovery.

The first step in the conservation effort was to remove thousands of wire snares and traps across the park. The next step was to bring back herbivores such as wildebeest, zebras, and buffalo.

After the herbivores were re-established, it was time for carnivores such as hyenas and leopards. The lion population recovered on its own as the ecosystem food webs naturally rebounded.

It did not take long for other wildlife populations to grow as well. After only a few years, the park went from having very few large animals to more than 100,000.

Part of Carr's vision included investing in the people who lived in the area. Following the war, many local people lived in extreme poverty, and the rewilded park provided many jobs. Tourists came to visit the park, which brought money and more jobs to the area. Carr also supported local efforts for improving education and healthcare.

A baboon in Gorongosa National Park
Credit: Thomas Shahan (CC BY 2.0)

Why invest in people as part of a conservation effort? If you include local people in conservation efforts, they are more likely to feel valued and part of the process. When the spiritual and cultural heritage of the community is recognized and honored, the people become part of supporting the park conservation and protection. The rewilding of Gorongosa National Park was so successful because local people were part of the effort.

> **Watch this full-length documentary, *Our Gorongosa: A Park for the People*, to learn about the conservation efforts at Gorongosa and the involvement of the local community.** Why do you think they call Gorongosa "a park for the people"?
>
> 🔍 Gorongosa film

CONSERVATION SUCCESS

WORDS TO KNOW

GPS collar: a collar placed on an animal that uses the Global Positioning System to track the animal.

A variety of technologies help the ongoing management, study, and protection of the park and its wildlife. A digital radio system enables communication across the more than 1,500 square miles of the park. **GPS collars** are also placed on at-risk species to monitor the animals' movements. GPS tracking allows rangers to minimize their interactions with wildlife, track poaching incidents, and enforce punishments. In addition, researchers have created a database of biodiversity in the park that has more than 1,500 different plant species and close to 100 newly discovered species of frogs, bats, and insects!

Due to the success at Gorongosa National Park, it has become a living classroom for scientists, locals, and students.

Gorongosa National Park

Credit: Judy Gallagher (CC BY 2.0)

Young Conservationist: Linh Nguyen (Vietnam)

As a fifth-grader, Linh Nguyen of Vietnam noticed changes in the environment. Instead of just worrying about the changes, Nguyen took action. In her words, "We need to turn thought into action—only through action can you solve the problems." Her work started when she asked principals to stop releasing balloons at their schools' opening ceremonies because the balloons ended up falling back to the ground as litter and harming wildlife and the environment.

At 12 years old, Nguyen and two of her friends wrote a book for kids called *A Piece of Forest for You*. She wanted to share her love of forests with kids living in cities who may not be able to visit a forest and see its importance. The book also explains why forests need protection. Nguyen donated more than $4,000 of the profits from sales of the book to the Forest Plantation Fund. In addition, Nguyen travels to festivals and schools to promote awareness about the value of forests. In 2022, Nguyen won the Vietnam Environment Award, the highest award given in Vietnam for environmental action. That same year, she also received an International Young Eco-Hero Award.

GO WILD

Rewilding efforts are also happening in unlikely places—in yards and neighborhoods, on golf courses, and even in cities. The term "urban rewilding" might seem strange, but this type of rewilding is a conservation effort aimed at reclaiming green spaces within towns and cities. Many cities even purposefully set aside spaces for community gardens or parks for rewilding. This rewilding effort is about increasing biodiversity with native plants, connecting natural areas when possible, and leaving space for wildlife.

March 20 is World Rewilding Day. Visit the Rewilding Europe website to learn more. How can you get involved in Rewilding Day?

⌕ World Rewilding Day

CONSERVATION SUCCESS

WORDS TO KNOW

rehabilitate: to restore something to its previous condition.

pesticide: a chemical used to kill pests such as rodents or insects.

microorganism: a living organism that is so small you can see it only with a microscope.

Abandoned golf courses are great places for rewilding. What do you notice about a golf course? It's very neat and even, isn't it? All the grass is trimmed and there's a lot of it, with very few trees or bushes interrupting the neat expanse of grass. And you won't spot much wildlife. When in use, these spaces are not good for the environment. They use a lot of water and energy to maintain and they aren't inviting to different species of plants, animals, and insects.

But what do you think happens when golf courses are abandoned? Nature moves back in! Some former golf courses require only a little assistance, such as removing ditches and restoring natural hydrology.

One way people are rewilding cities is by creating green roofs! These roofs are topped with soil and planted with native plants and even trees—providing great habitats for birds and insects.

Species Spotlight: Pangolins

Many of the local people around Gorongosa now work as wildlife rangers and protect the park. Their work includes keeping endangered pangolins safe. Poachers catch, transport, and kill these animals for their scales. In some traditional medicine, pangolin scales are believed to have healing and magical properties, so there is a huge demand for them in illegal trade. As a result, the first pangolin rescue program in Mozambique was established at Gorongosa. When rescued pangolins are brought in, they are treated, protected, and **rehabilitated**. The goal is to return them to the wild in secure locations. Scientists track these pangolins with satellite technology to monitor their health and survival.

Rewilding golf courses might also involve removing non-native grasses and plants and replacing them with native ones. The rewilded space may serve as a connection between parks and wild places.

Many homeowners are even rewilding their yards. That means replacing lawns with native plants, not mowing or raking, and not using **pesticides** or fertilizers. Even in small yards, these rewilded spaces create habitats for birds, insects, and **microorganisms** and increase biodiversity.

Rewildology **has a regular podcast that shares stories about the world's wildest places.** Many of those podcasts focus on rewilding. Choose an episode to listen to here! Why do you think it is important to share stories of wilderness and rewilding around the world?

🔍 *Rewildology* podcast

In the United States, the presence of darter fish is an indicator of a river's health.

As with all conservation efforts, the benefits of rewilding extend beyond nature to people. Rewilded spaces within urban areas and neighborhoods allow people to reconnect with nature and find calm and quiet in a busy world. This connection is good for mental health as well as physical health. It's also good for nature because people sometimes get inspired to take a role in conservation.

ESSENTIAL QUESTION

How is rewilding an effective approach to conservation?

Have you been to any rewilded areas? How do they make you feel?

The restoration and rewilding conservation efforts you've read about so far have focused on whole ecosystems. In the next chapter, you will read about efforts focused on reintroducing a single species.

TEXT TO **WORLD**

Look around at some of the lawns, parks, and golf courses in your neighborhood. What would be different if these places were wild?

MAKE
SEED BOMBS

You do not have to own a castle or a national park to be part of rewilding! This type of conservation effort can be done on a much smaller scale—even your own yard or neighborhood park. Where to start? Launch a wildflower seed bomb! If you utilize seeds of plants native to your area, you will be promoting biodiversity.

❯ **Put three handfuls of clay and five handfuls of soil into the bucket.** Add water and mix together with your hands. Get dirty! Keep adding water until the mixture feels like cookie dough.

❯ **Add a handful of seeds to the bucket.** Mix well.

❯ **Divide the mixture and roll it into balls about the size of a golf ball.**

❯ **Roll each ball in dry soil to coat.** Do this a few more times. The extra layer of soil protects the seeds from insects or birds.

❯ **Set the seed bombs out to dry.** It will take several days, depending on the humidity in your area.

❯ **Find appropriate areas to launch your seed bomb.** This might be your own yard, on the school grounds, or any place that looks like it might need rewilding. Before launching, be sure to get permission from the property owner!

❯ **Prepare for launch.** The best time of year is early spring, right before a rainfall. Decide how you will launch them. You can use a catapult, lacrosse stick, or even your hands.

❯ **Launch your bombs!**

Try This!

Keep a record of where you launch your seed bombs. You may want to take a "before" photo of the area. Revisit the sites throughout the season to watch the seeds grow and take an "after" photo.

MEASURING
DIVERSITY

Biodiversity includes all living species, from the largest plants to the smallest microorganisms and everything in between—animals, insects, fungi, flowers, and more. So how do scientists measure biodiversity in an area? They do a biodiversity survey. To better understand the process, do a survey in an area near you.

❯ **Randomly place your hula hoop or marker on the ground in a natural area outside.**

❯ **Take notes about the environment outside of your marked area.** Sketch what you see. Don't forget trees, water sources, fences, walkways, etc. If you know the names of plants and trees, label them.

❯ **Note the weather, including temperature, cloud cover, and humidity.**

❯ **Now, look inside your marked area.** How many different species of plants and animals can you see? Record your findings. If you do not know a species, sketch it and include a description so you can research it later.

❯ **Count the number of species you recorded—that's the species richness in that area.**

Try This!

Do a survey in several spots in the same general area. How does the biodiversity within the different marked areas compare? Are there more species? Fewer? Why do you think the number of species varies from spot to spot within the same general area?

Chapter 3

DISCOVER

REINTRODUCTION

At first, reintroduction might seem the same as rewilding. And yes, they are similar. But they're not the same! In the last chapter, you read about rewilding, which often involves bringing various wildlife or plants back to an area that was degraded or destroyed. Rewilding and restoration focus on the whole ecosystem. Reintroduction, however, focuses on returning one species to an area from which it has disappeared.

ESSENTIAL QUESTION

Why is it important to reintroduce species to ecosystems?

Reintroduction usually focuses on endangered or **threatened species**. Scientists reintroduce a species to a place where it once lived in an attempt to boost its population in the wild. Reintroductions have other benefits—they rebuild food webs, increase biodiversity, and make ecosystems stronger and more resilient. Let's look at some examples.

CANADA LYNX IN COLORADO

Canada lynx once prowled throughout the Rocky Mountains, from Canada into Colorado. Their story is like that of many animals. European settlers moved westward in the 1800s and trapped lynx for their fur. Logging, and the expansion of towns and cities, also reduced lynx populations. In addition, predators such as lynx were trapped and poisoned in an effort to protect livestock.

In Colorado, lynx sightings became increasingly rare. The last lynx in Colorado was killed in 1974. During the 1990s, people at what was then called the Colorado Division of Wildlife (DOW) asked a question.

Canada lynx have large, fur-covered paws that spread out wide and work like snowshoes so the lynx can walk on powdery snow.

A Canada Lynx
Credit: Art G. (CC BY 2.0)

If humans were responsible for eliminating the lynx in Colorado, could they bring it back?

Soon, that what-if idea became a reality. DOW assembled a team of people, including researchers and biologists, who were passionate about reintroducing the lynx to the state.

Next, it created a conservation strategy with other agencies, including the U.S. Fish and Wildlife Service (USFWS), the National Forest Service, and the NPS. One part of that conservation strategy was to identify a suitable habitat that included plenty of the lynx's favorite prey—snowshoe hares. The goal became to establish a self-sustaining population of lynx in the southern Rockies.

In 1999, five lynx were trapped in Canada and transported to a facility in Colorado. After a veterinary exam, each was fitted with a radio collar so the team could track it. The lynx were released into the mountains as onlookers cheered.

The endangered red panda

IUCN Red List

The International Union for the Conservation of Nature (IUCN) Red List of Threatened Species is a record of species of plants, animals, and fungi around the world. It lists species based on their status in the wild. Species listed as "Least Concern" are not threatened at all. Other categories are "Near Threatened," "Vulnerable," and "Endangered." Species listed as "Critically Endangered" are at a high risk for **extinction** in the wild. The last two categories on the list are "Extinct in the Wild" and "Extinct."

The various categories allow scientists to understand the risks different species face. Conservationists, scientists, and governments also use the categories to guide their efforts to help species that are in trouble.

Watch the video on the IUCN website to learn more about the list of categories and what the organization does. Do you think it is important to have such a list of plants, animals, and fungi around the world?

🔎 IUCN Red List history

But . . . those cheers soon turned into despair. Some of the lynx died—they had starved to death. The news was devastating, but the scientists learned from it. They held the next group of lynx at the facility for more than three weeks and fed them a high-calorie diet. They released the lynx into the wild after April 1, when prey was most abundant. Every time the scientists made adjustments to the way they reintroduced the lynx, the lynx survival rate increased.

Scientists still monitor the lynx in Colorado to make sure they are healthy.

To create a self-sustaining population in Colorado, the lynx had to **reproduce** in their new home. The team waited. And waited. And waited. Finally, in May 2003: kittens! And not just in one den. The team discovered six dens with a total of 16 kittens. As time went on, more than 200 lynx were reintroduced in the state. The lynx continued to reproduce and established a self-sustaining population. Success!

EURASIAN BEAVERS

Roots and Shoots is an organization that encourages youth to get involved, make a difference, and create change. Learn how you can get started. How can you make a positive impact in your community?

🔎 Roots Shoots

In Chapter 1, you met the beavers of North America. Eurasian beavers are their close cousins. Once upon a time, they lived across Europe and parts of Asia. And, like their North American relatives, they were hunted nearly to extinction.

Several countries in Europe first reintroduced Eurasian beavers during the 1900s. Serbia joined the effort in the early twenty-first century. The Reintroduction of the Eurasian Beaver project started in 2004 in partnership with an environmental organization in Germany that donated the beavers following its own success with reintroduction.

CONSERVATION SUCCESS

As with all species, though, you don't just pick up a few beavers, move them, and hope for the best. A lot of research goes into selecting the right location. In Serbia, the Zasavica Special Nature Reserve was chosen for historical, biological, and ecological reasons. Eurasian beavers had lived in the region for 15,000 years! Zasavica has wetlands and a river as well as plenty of food for beavers.

Scientists also considered the **territorial** needs of the Eurasian beavers. The first beavers brought from Germany were part of four different families. Within the reserve, the families were placed 3 miles apart to give each family enough territory. Serbia took care to protect the new residents by regularly patrolling the area and issuing hefty fines for harming beavers.

A Eurasian beaver

Credit: NasserHalaweh (CC BY-SA 4.0)

Zasavica Special Nature Reserve

Credit: Snowyns (CC BY-SA 4.0)

The scientists chose well. The beavers settled right in and built new dams. They even **dispersed** along the Zasavica bog and beyond—another good sign that the beavers were where they needed to be. Finally, the beavers had young!

Beavers' teeth are orange because they have iron in the enamel—this makes their teeth super strong and able to chew through tree trunks.

At the beginning of the project, the reintroduced beavers were **microchipped** so scientists could monitor their movement. The population rebounded so well that the government stopped funding the tracking system. Scientists estimate that as of 2022, there were as many as 3,000 Eurasian beavers in Serbia.

The Eurasian beaver was also reintroduced to locations in Great Britain, Spain, Central Europe, Scandinavia, Mongolia, and China. Now, the Eurasian beaver is no longer critically endangered and is considered a species of least concern, which means the species is thriving.

Read more stories about the reintroduction of endangered species around the world. Which reintroduction would you like to be involved in? Why?

🔍 Weforum endangered species

WORDS TO KNOW

mammal: a type of animal, such as a human, dog, or cat. Mammals are born live, feed milk to their young, and usually have hair or fur covering most of their skin.

larva: the wormlike stage of an insect's life. The plural is larvae.

secretion: a fluid produced by an organism.

pupate: to turn into a pupa, one stage of an insect's life cycle.

BRINGING BACK THE BUTTERFLIES

Mammals are not the only species being reintroduced—insects are, too!

Meet large blue, a beautiful blue butterfly once found across Europe and parts of Asia. Large blue is categorized as "Near Threatened" on the IUCN's Red List of Threatened Species. It became extinct in the United Kingdom in 1979.

This story of reintroduction involves the large blue butterfly, ants, cows, and a camper van. When scientists first considered reintroducing large blues to the United Kingdom, they knew they first needed to understand its complex life cycle. That required a bit of detective work.

In the United States, twenty-first-century insect conservation efforts include the reintroduction of the American burying beetle, Puritan tiger beetle, and Mission blue butterfly.

PLANTS, ANIMALS, AND INSECTS ALL FIT TOGETHER LIKE PUZZLE PIECES.

WHEN ALL THE PIECES FALL INTO PLACE . . .

. . . THEY HELP EACH OTHER SURVIVE AND THRIVE!

It took British professor of ecology Jeremy Thomas years of fieldwork. To unravel the mystery of the large blue's lifecycle, he collected data, counted eggs, and determined how ants figured into the story.

Learn more about the different ways the Butterfly Conservation is protecting moths and butterflies. Why is this often a very complex process?

🔍 Butterfly Conservation

The life of a large blue butterfly begins when an egg is laid on a flower bud of wild thyme. The **larva** then burrows into the flower head to feed. When it is still smaller than a grain of rice, the larva drops to the ground. This is where the ants come in. But not just any ant—it must be one particular species, *Myrmica sabuleti*.

The butterfly larvae produce a sweet-smelling **secretion** to attract those red ants. Not only that, the larvae "sing" to the ants! This tricks the ants into thinking the butterfly larvae are queen ant grubs. The ants then carry the larvae like royalty into their underground chambers. If only the ants knew that those larvae would later feed on their grubs all winter long! The large blue larvae stay in the ant nest, **pupate** there, and then emerge as adult butterflies.

A large blue butterfly

Credit: gailhampshire (CC BY 2.0)

CONSERVATION SUCCESS

WORDS TO KNOW

Endangered Species Act (ESA): a law in the United States that identifies threatened and endangered species. The listed species are protected and their habitats are conserved.

What this all means is that scientists needed both wild thyme and red ants to reintroduce the butterflies. That involved research about suitable habitats and plans for managing the habitat. Apparently, *Myrmica sabuleti* are rather picky, too. The ants needed grazed grass, which maintains a certain soil temperature. Enter cows. The grazers recreated the perfect conditions for both ant and butterfly.

In 1983, after the perfect site was located, the first large blue butterfly caterpillars were brought via camper van to the United Kingdom from Sweden.

Jeremy Thomas's thorough research paid off. More large blue butterflies are now in the United Kingdom than ever before recorded—it's the largest large blue population in the world.

Young Conservationist: Tao "Ty" Le Marchand (United States)

Ty Le Marchand (2012–) loves wolves. As a preteen, he raised money to donate to a wolf sanctuary in Pennsylvania. But he worried about the wolves in Yellowstone when they were taken off the list of endangered species in 2021. Because they were no longer on the list, they could be hunted.

Le Marchand wrote to the president of the United States to ask him to relist wolves so they would be protected by the **Endangered Species Act (ESA)**. Then, he began another fundraising campaign to raise money for the Yellowstone Wolf Project to help monitor the wolves in the park. He created a flyer to give to friends and neighbors and encouraged people to learn about wolves and their role in ecosystems. Le Marchand believes that kids have great ideas and should be involved in helping the environment. As of 2022, most but not all gray wolf populations in the lower 48 states were relisted and protected under the ESA.

Myrmica sabuleti

Not only that, but the restored habitats also support other endangered plants and animals such as the pasqueflower, the shrill carder bee, the Downland villa bee-fly, and eight endangered species of butterflies. The large blue butterfly conservation efforts continue at different sites to this day.

These reintroductions are just one way conservationists are supporting individual species. In the next chapter, you'll learn more about how scientists are recovering the populations of endangered and threatened species.

Watch scientists celebrate the return of the large blue butterfly in Gloucestershire, England.
What role does hope play in conservation efforts?

🔎 National Trust Rodborough butterfly

ESSENTIAL QUESTION

Why is it important to reintroduce species to ecosystems?

TEXT TO **WORLD**

What endangered species do you feel a strong connection to? Why?

MAKE A HOME
FOR MICROORGANISMS

In ecosystems, each species, including microorganisms, has its own role. Create a habitat for microorganisms called a Winogradsky column, named after Russian microbiologist Sergei Winogradsky (1856–1953). Watch the microorganisms in your habitat to see how they interact.

❯ **Cut off the top, curved part of the bottle.** Shred or cut the newspaper into small pieces. Crack the egg and separate the yolk from the white. Put the yolk in the small bowl. Discard the white part.

❯ **In the large bucket, collect enough mud from a riverbank, mud puddle, or pond to fill the plastic bottle.** Use the shovel to remove all solid materials from the mud—rocks, twigs, etc. Be careful to watch for broken glass and sharp objects.

❯ **Add water to the mud and stir until it is about as thick as a milkshake.** Put ¼ of the mud mix into the smaller bucket. Add a handful of newspaper bits and the egg yolk to the smaller bucket. Stir. The newspaper will provide carbon and the yolk will provide sulfur for your microbes.

❯ **Fill the bottle with the mud-newspaper-egg mixture until it is about a quarter full.** Tap the bottom of the bottle on a hard surface to remove pockets of air and allow the mud mix to settle. Add the plain mud mixture from the large bucket until the bottle is 3/4 full. Again, tap the bottle to remove air and allow the mud to settle. Add water until it fills to 1 inch below the top edge of the bottle.

IDEAS FOR SUPPLIES

- 2-liter plastic bottle
- page of newspaper
- 1 egg
- small bowl
- mud
- water
- spoon
- plastic wrap
- rubber band (large enough to fit around the wide part of the plastic bottle)
- small spade
- two buckets (one large and one medium)
- science journal

AN EGG

MUD

A SPADE

WATER

A RUBBER BAND

SHREDDED NEWSPAPER

AN OLD EMPTY BOTTLE

48

❯ **Stretch the plastic wrap over the top of the bottle and use the rubber band to keep it in place.** Put your column in a sunny location. Take a photo or draw a picture of your column.

❯ **Observe the column daily for the next several weeks and record what you see.** Are there microbes moving? Separating? Are layers forming? Each week at the same time, take or draw a new picture.

❯ **After 8 to 10 weeks, research the microbes that may be in your column based on where they are in the mud.** Oxygen levels will be highest at the top of the column, and sulfur levels will be highest at the bottom. The different colors will give you clues about the microorganisms in the column.

Try This!

Repeat the experiment and create two to three different columns at the same time. Use mud from the same source but vary the amount of sunlight each one gets. Or put only newspaper in one column and only egg yolk in the other. An alternative is to vary the sources of mud but keep all other factors the same. What similarities do the columns have after 8 to 10 weeks? What differences?

MAKE A
WATER FILTER

Beavers are keystone species and ecosystem engineers. Their dams create new wetland habitats that are important to both biodiversity and water quality. Wetlands are natural water filters. Witness the natural process by making your own water filter.

NOTE: No not drink your clean water even if it looks clear!

❯ **Have an adult help you cut the bottom off the plastic bottle.** Turn the bottle upside down and place it so the spout of the bottle will empty into the jar.

❯ **Layer the filter materials (gravel, sand, cotton balls) in the plastic bottle.** Consider how to filter larger objects out first and smaller particles last. Decide in what order the materials should go.

❯ **Pour the dirty water in the top of your filter.** Wait for the filtered water to drip into the jar, and then evaluate your filter. How does the filtered water look compared to the dirty water? Does it smell different? Feel different?

IDEAS FOR SUPPLIES

- clear, disposable, plastic bottle
- clear glass jar
- gravel
- sand
- cotton balls
- dirty water (find or even make some—water with visible particles is best)
- science journal

Try This!

Examine your dirty water through a microscope. Then, look at a sample of the filtered water. Do you see a difference? Try making filters with different materials to improve and slow the filtering process. Compare the results.

Chapter 4

SPECIES
RECOVERY

George and Martha were the last of their kind. When they passed away, the world suffered an enormous loss. We are not talking about the first president of the United States and his wife here. We're talking about two animals that were the last of their species. Lonesome George, native to the Galapagos Islands, was the last Pinta Island tortoise on Earth. He died in 2012. Martha was a passenger pigeon living in the Cincinnati Zoo. She passed away almost 100 years earlier, in 1914.

ESSENTIAL QUESTION

Why is the recovery of an individual species an important part of conservation?

George and Martha represent only two of many species that are now extinct. Scientists around the world work tirelessly to prevent more extinctions. They hope to recover the population of a species before it is too late.

CONSERVATION SUCCESS

Sometimes, **captive breeding** is used to recover a species. With help from scientists, animals are bred in a safe place and then reintroduced to their natural habitat. Other times, people work to recover a species by protecting its habitats, passing laws to protect the species, banning the use of harmful pesticides, or removing invasive species. In some cases, entire organizations are dedicated to one species, such as the group Save the Elephants!

Other times, people use a combination of strategies to recover a species. No matter the approach, the goal is to prevent the worst—extinction—from happening.

CAPTIVE BREEDING

Do you live in an area with lots of frogs? Imagine you notice fewer and fewer frogs where you once spotted many. You're concerned they might disappear altogether. So, what do you do? You start a frog hotel!

That is exactly what happened in Panama. In 2006, Panamanian biologist Edgardo Griffith noticed a concerning decline in Panamanian golden frogs. The frogs were dying because of a deadly **fungus** that had already wiped out many other **amphibian** species in Central America.

Every year on August 14, the people of Panama have a festival to celebrate Golden Frog Day! In 2023, someone even wrote a song in the frogs' honor, "La Rana Dorada," which translates to "The Golden Frog." You can listen to it here. How can the arts play a role in conservation?

🔎 EVACC Foundation

PS

A golden frog

Credit: Brian Gratwicke (CC BY 2.0)

He was desperate to save the golden frog, a symbol of good luck in Panama. Griffith called on biologists, environmentalists, and zookeepers. They trudged through the rainforests at night, collecting as many golden frogs as they could. The hotel ended up with more than 300 guests, including golden frogs and other threatened amphibians.

Placing animals in captivity might not sound like you're saving them. Yet, done properly, captivity can keep a species from going extinct. In the hotel, the frogs were regularly cleaned, monitored, and fed well. They got room service 24 hours a day! And filtered water! The frogs were hosted in a hotel until El Valle Amphibian Conservation Center (EVACC) was completed the next year. The center now houses and breeds golden frogs as well as other amphibians in the area that are facing extinction. Scientists hope to find a cure for the fungus and reintroduce the frogs to the wild one day.

Learn more about the ongoing research and conservation efforts of EVACC on their website. What role does EVACC play in species recovery in Central America?

⌕ EVACC Foundation

WORDS TO KNOW

gene: a section of DNA that codes for a particular trait. DNA stands for deoxyribonucleic acid, the substance found in cells that carries genes, the genetic information that contains the blueprint of an organism.

trait: a specific characteristic of an organism determined by genes or the environment.

offspring: an animal's young.

Watch this TedEd video to learn about the role of zoos in saving the last true wild horse, known to Mongolians as takhi. Are the reintroduced takhi truly wild?

🔍 TedEd takhi

ZOOS AND AQUARIUMS

Like EVACC, zoos and aquariums are key to keeping many animal species from going extinct. In these places, people are not simply holding animals in pens, cages, terrariums, or tanks so that we can look at them. They are playing matchmaker in captive breeding programs to maintain a species' genetic diversity.

On Ice

One effort to save species has no live species at all. They are frozen! The Frozen Zoo, part of the San Diego Zoo Wildlife Alliance, houses collections of genetic material from more than 1,000 different species. The Frozen Zoo is similar to a bank. The genetic material is deposited and saved for the future. It even has material from one extinct species, the po'ouli, a bird once native to Hawaii. Scientists could potentially use the genetic material stored at the Frozen Zoo to produce new offspring of a species.

Watch this episode of *CBS News Sunday Morning* about using DNA to try to save species from extinction. What do you think about trying to bring back already extinct species?

🔍 CBS de-extinction

Genes determine the **traits** that **offspring** inherit from their parents. Genes influence behavior, looks, and the way an organism grows. With more genetic diversity, a species is better able to adapt to changes in its environment and fight off disease. The population is stronger and the species has a better chance for long-term survival.

A species with fewer individual organisms is a species with less genetic diversity. That's where zoos and aquariums and their captive breeding programs come in.

Early zoos were places for people to see animals kept in cages. During the early 1900s, zoos began to replace cages with habitats that tried to mimic what the animals had in the wild. Then, in the mid-1900s, the mission of many zoos turned to conservation and captive breeding.

Zoos and aquariums keep detailed records of individual endangered animals in captivity around the world. The data includes an animal's age, gender, family history, genetic makeup, and more. Using computer software and data, scientists create plans for the survival of a species.

A tiger lounging at the San Diego Zoo

Credit: Jim1138 (CC BY-SA 3.0)

55

Scientists also use data to find the best possible mates for individual animals. Once they make a match, they transport one of the animals to meet the other. Then, everyone waits, hoping the pair will get along and eventually breed. Scientists organize this kind of matchmaking for rhinos, penguins, sloths, porcupines, warthogs, polar bears, monkeys, and more.

CAPTIVE BREEDING SUCCESS STORIES

A California condor

Credit: Grand Canyon National Park (CC BY 2.0)

California Condor

By 1987, fewer than 30 California condors were left in the wild. The species had been wiped out by lead poisoning! When the condors ate dead animals that had been shot with lead bullets, the condors died of lead poisoning. The USFWS decided the best way to save them was to capture them all. Breeding and a ban on lead bullets saved the species. As of 2024, more than 500 California condors are in the wild.

Mussels in the Licking River

This river in Kentucky had lost several of its native species of mussels due to poor water quality. But through captive breeding and reintroduction, six species were recovered in that ecosystem.

The Licking River

Credit: James St. John (CC BY 2.0)

A Wollemi pine
Credit: Amanda Slater (CC BY-SA 2.0)

Wollemi Pine

This conifer in Australia is one of the rarest in the world, with fewer than 100 growing in the wild. Conservationists work to increase the genetic diversity of the Wollemi pine by growing new trees in botanical gardens. Plus, private citizens grow these trees in their own gardens.

Golden Lion Tamarin

By the 1970s, only a few hundred of these small monkeys were left in the wild. Then, more than 100 zoos joined the effort to begin captive breeding programs. As of 2020, more than 3,000 golden lion tamarins were in the wild.

A golden lion tamarin
Credit: Mab Shoot (CC BY 2.0)

Black-Footed Ferret

The black-footed ferret, which once thrived in the plains and mountain regions of the western United States, was thought to be extinct. But in the 1980s, scientists found a small colony and later captured it. Several zoos and the National Black-Footed Ferret Conservation Center created breeding programs, eventually reintroduced the ferrets to their native habitats, and then monitored them. As of 2023, more than 400 ferrets survived in the wild.

A black-footed ferret
Credit: U.S. Department of Agriculture (CC BY 2.0)

RECOVERING SPECIES IN THE FIELD

We've looked at how captive breeding programs help recover some species. What about conservation efforts that happen in the wild?

Many sea turtle species are threatened or endangered. One way to recover populations of sea turtles is through laws and protections, which we'll discuss more in Chapter 8. Another way involves trying to reduce the number of turtle deaths that result from them getting tangled in fishing gear. Also, many organizations ask people to help turtles by turning off outdoor lights and closing window shades at night so beaches remain dark. Artificial light can confuse a nesting female turtle and even keep her from laying eggs. Plus, dark beaches prevent hatchlings from skittering inland instead of toward the ocean.

Witness a baby turtle's first steps in this video! What are some of the challenges these turtles face as they age?

🔍 BBC Earth baby turtles hatch

Hand-on efforts all over the world protect turtle nesting beaches. In Florida, the state, the USFWS, conservation organizations, and volunteers work to protect turtles from April to October, which is turtle breeding season. One thing they do is improve the beaches. Starting an hour before sunrise, people patrol the beaches every morning and remove obstacles such as mounds, trash, and boats so the turtles have a clear path back to the ocean. Volunteers also fill in holes and educate the public about the turtles and their nests.

On the Galapagos Islands, 136 tortoises were raised in captivity and released with the hope that their role as ecosystem engineers will repair the ecosystem and increase biodiversity.

In addition, volunteers look for turtle tracks—trails in the sand where females hauled themselves out of the water and onto the beach to dig a hole and lay their eggs. If volunteers find a nest, they mark it and put a screen over it to protect the eggs from predators.

Young Conservationists: Waterfowl Conservation (United States)

Sometimes, a duck just needs a helping hand. And that is exactly what students at an elementary school in Butte, Montana, offered. In partnership with biologists from Montana Wetlands and Waterfowl, students built structures called hen houses for ducks to nest in.

The structures are made of hay sandwiched between garden fencing and then rolled to create a tube. The finished hen house tubes are approximately 3 feet long and 11 to 12 inches in diameter. Out in the wetlands, the hen houses are attached to poles a few feet off the ground. Many of the students enjoyed rolling nest burritos instead of doing math. Plus, they got a real-life, hands-on lesson in conservation and making a difference right in their own backyard.

WORDS TO KNOW

eradicate: to eliminate, remove, or destroy something.

Volunteers record data about the nest and its location and monitor the nest for the next 50 to 60 days as the eggs incubate. When the eggs hatch, volunteers count the number of hatchlings and make sure each hatchling makes it safely to the water. Scientists use all this data to improve their conservation efforts and keep track of sea turtle numbers.

On the other side of the world, a different type of threat—invasive species—faced the kākāpō. These flightless birds are a parrot species that once thrived in the forests of New Zealand until settlers introduced stoats, feral cats, dogs, and rats to the country.

Because they don't fly, the kākāpō were an easy meal for these new predators. Humans hunted the kākāpō, too. Their numbers dropped.

Conservation Canines

Conservation has a non-human ally in saving species—dogs! After extensive training, dogs assist scientists in the field. They can smell things humans can't—a valuable tool for locating everything from specific animal species to viruses and scat to trace evidence of insects.

Dogs and their human partners work together. The dogs learn to track a certain scent, then the pair sets out on a job. When they find what they're looking for, they retrieve samples for scientists. These samples provide critical information about species population, health, and location.

The first attempt to save the kākāpō was in 1894, when several hundred birds were moved to an island free from predators. But it was only a matter of time before stoats arrived and wiped out the birds on the island.

In the mid-1900s, the kākāpō were moved to different islands, but the predators continued to be a problem. Finally, beginning in 1980, scientists formed a new plan—to **eradicate** the invasive species from the kākāpō's sanctuary islands. As stoats, feral cats, dogs, and rats were removed from these islands, hope for the kākāpō grew. From only 51 birds in 1995, the numbers rose to 62 by 2000, then to more than 200 in 2023. These numbers continue to rise, and scientists are working to restore the kākāpō to more of their natural range.

Visit this website, Species in Pieces, to learn about 30 endangered species and the threats they face. Why do you think the creators chose this format for the exhibit? Is it effective?

🔎 Species Pieces

The hope people felt in New Zealand about the kākāpō is the reason so many people are dedicated to species recovery. That hope and dedication, combined with research and science, result in successful conservation.

And hope is also the reason people work to reconnect wildlife habitats. We'll learn more about this type of conservation in the next chapter.

ESSENTIAL QUESTION

Why is the recovery of an individual species an important part of conservation?

PLANTS AND
POLLUTED WATER

Polluted water is a threat to many species of plants and animals. Water can become polluted by trash, pesticides, factory waste, **sewage**, and more. In some cases, changes in the water's **acidity** or temperature result in harmful microorganisms. Polluted water can be toxic or harm plant and animal species. See for yourself how plants absorb polluted water.

NOTE: If you want to use a fertilizer or pesticide in your experiment, ask an adult for help.

❯ **Fill each jar with ½ cup of water.** Set one jar aside—this is your control.

❯ **Add a teaspoon of one pollutant to each of the other jars.** Label each jar so you remember which pollutant is in which jar. Place one flower in each jar, including the control jar.

❯ **Wait 24 hours.** Observe the petals and stems of each flower. Record your findings.

✳ What happened to them? How did the different pollutants affect the flowers?

✳ How did they compare to the control jar that did not have a pollutant?

✳ What can you conclude about the different pollutants and how they affect plants in the ecosystem?

Try This!

Repeat the experiment using water from different sources—tap water, filtered water, and water from several different natural sources near you (a pond, stream, ditch, ocean, or wetland). What happens to the flowers in these different types of water? Which did the best? Which the worst? What does this information tell you about the water supply in your area?

WORDS TO KNOW

sewage: waste from buildings carried away through sewers.

acidity: the level of acids in a substance such as water and soil. Examples include vinegar and lemon juice.

FIGHT AGAINST
INVASIVE SPECIES

IDEAS FOR SUPPLIES

- internet access
- science journal
- posterboard
- markers or colored pencils

Ecosystems are well-balanced systems and any invasive species can cause harm. For some native plants and animals, an invasive species can put them at risk for extinction. Invasive species are a problem worldwide, even near you. Find out more about an invasive plant species in your area.

❯ **Research an invasive plant species in your area, where it occurs, how it is harming native species, and what is being done.**

❯ **If possible, visit an area to see the plant firsthand.** It may even be found in your own yard or nearby park. Take pictures or draw what you see.

This NPS video discusses the differences between native and non-native species and between invasive species and pests. In what ways do invasive species disrupt ecosystems? Why aren't these species a problem in their natural ecosystem?

🔎 NPS invasive species

❯ **Record your observations about where it grows and the native species growing around it.**

❯ **Create an "Unwanted" poster to increase awareness about the invasive plant.** Include information about what people can do to help control the plant in their own yards and local volunteer opportunities.

Try This!

There are likely invasive insects in your area, too. Repeat the above activity but focus on an invasive insect. Spread the word about invasive insects in your neighborhood and how individuals can help eradicate them.

TEXT TO WORLD

Have you visited a zoo? Did the animals there seem well cared for?

Chapter 5

HABITAT

RECONNECTION

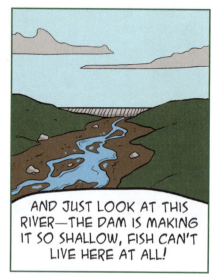

Animals move. They slither, hop, fly, swim, walk, crawl, trek, wriggle, and migrate in search of shelter, food, water, and mates. All this movement is important to their survival. But what happens if their route is blocked by a road or dam? What happens if their wilderness is turned into a neighborhood? Or if the habitat they relied on along their migration route disappears?

ESSENTIAL QUESTION

Why is it important to reconnect wild spaces on land and in the water?

Earth was once a vast wilderness of interconnected ecosystems. But as time passed, wild spaces disappeared. Roads, farms, dams, and urban development **fragmented** ecosystems. Habitats were destroyed, leaving **habitat islands** and blocked migration routes. For wildlife, movement across their natural ranges became dangerous or even impossible. It could be harder for animals to find enough food.

In addition, genetic diversity drops because animals can't find new mates or reach spawning grounds. As genetic diversity drops, so does the health and adaptability of species.

To fix this, many conservation efforts focus on reconnecting habitats. People are linking parks and protected wilderness areas to create larger spaces and corridors for wildlife to travel between habitats. They're building special bridges and tunnels so animals do not have to cross busy roads. And they are removing obstacles such as dams so fish can migrate. Connected landscapes create safe passages. Let's look at some examples of this type of conservation.

NATURAL CORRIDORS

One way to reconnect fragmented habitats is by creating natural wildlife corridors. Scientists do this by identifying key pathways for wildlife between isolated habitats. In some places, they must restore corridors to link two natural habitats. In other places, they must create corridors by setting aside and protecting land or waterways. Partnerships between local, state, and federal governments, Native tribes, and private landowners are key to creating and managing the corridors.

Started in 2003, the European Greenbelt is an extensive wildlife corridor that involves more than 20 countries. It runs north to south across the continent of Europe for more than 7,765 miles.

Newly connected habitats can be small, single projects, such as a community creating a connection between local parks, gardens, and woodlands. They can also span a continent and involve multiple projects.

CONSERVATION SUCCESS

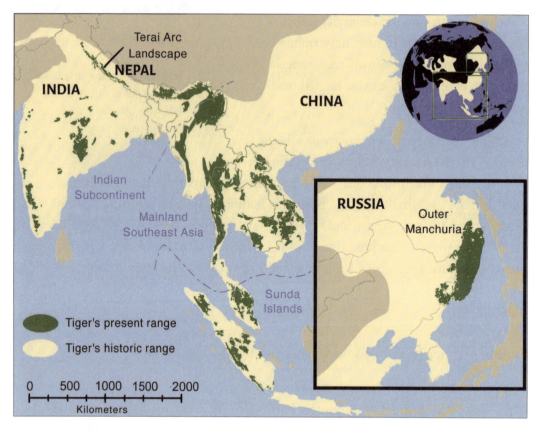

This map compares the current and historic ranges of tigers in Asia. By working together, countries can offer more protection to the species that need it.

Credit: Sanderson, E.; Forrest, J.; Loucks, C.; Ginsberg, J.; Dinerstein, E.; Seidensticker, J.; Leimgruber, P.; Songer, M.; Heydlauff, A.; O'Brien, T.; Bryja, G.; Klenzendorf, S.; Wikramanayake, E. (CC BY-SA 2.5)

Terai Arc Landscape in Asia is a massive conservation effort to reconnect habitats. This landscape straddles the border between Nepal and India. The river valleys, forests, wetlands, and grasslands provide critical habitat for tigers and many other large mammals such as elephants and rhinos. Each of the protected areas within the region was not big enough to support self-sustaining populations alone.

The Florida Wildlife Corridor Act became law in 2021 to conserve wilderness and save the state's declining wildlife. Visit the website to see the map of Florida's wildlife corridors. What animals are supported by these corridors?

Florida wildlife corridor map

The idea to link protected areas to allow wildlife to move across greater ranges formed in the Nepali government during the early 2000s, as an effort to protect tigers and increase their numbers. In partnership with India and the World Wildlife Fund, Nepal created natural corridors by focusing on forest restoration.

The government worked with local people to help protect against poaching by gathering data and acting as ecosystem stewards.

Visit American Bird Conservancy's website to see a map and learn more about flyways in the United States. Why do you think the flyways go north to south instead of west to east?

🔍 ABC four flyways

The Terai Arc now spans nearly 20,000 square miles, allowing tigers and other animals to travel safely to new habitats. It consists of more than a dozen different protected areas stretching across more than 500 miles. As of 2024, the number of tigers had doubled since the project's beginning.

Camera Traps

Camera traps are valuable tools in many conservation efforts because they allow scientists to be in many places at one time. Data is collected quickly and includes digital records that scientists can analyze.

When the cameras sense movement, they snap a picture. In wildlife conservation, the images provide valuable information about where, when, and what type of wildlife is in an area. The images can also be used to determine the population size, health, and habits of a species. All this data helps determine where wildlife crossings would be useful.

WORDS TO KNOW

WORDS TO KNOW

flyway: an air route used by migrating birds.

vernal pool: a shallow depression in the ground that holds water for part of the year and provides a habitat for animals and plants.

THE BIRDS AND THE BEES

Even birds and bees need connected habitats. You're probably thinking, "But they can fly! Can't they just fly to find food and mates?" In some cases, that is true. Elsewhere, habitats are so degraded that areas with food and safe shelter might be too far apart.

For migrating birds, **flyways** are critical. These are highways for those with wings! Flyways connect birds' breeding grounds to their wintering grounds. The Americas Flyway Initiative is a massive international effort to conserve critical habitats along flyways in North, Central, and South America. Conservationists identify key habitats for migrating birds along the flyways and restore, protect, and manage them.

For the bees, the people of Oslo, Norway, created a bee highway in 2014! Public officials as well as private urban gardeners got involved in planting meadows, flowers, and plants that bees need in strategic places across the city. Many mini habitats were in parks. People replaced manicured lawns with native flowers and grasses. Some were even placed in home and business rooftop gardens!

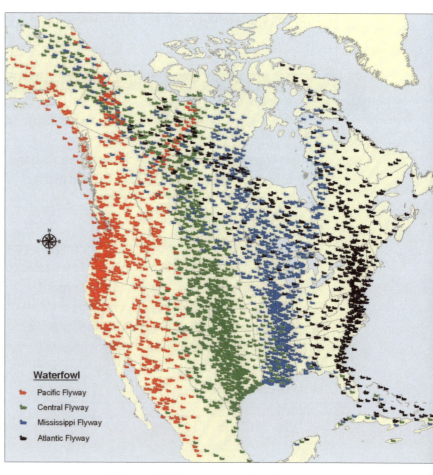

Waterfowl
- Pacific Flyway
- Central Flyway
- Mississippi Flyway
- Atlantic Flyway

Migratory bird patterns over North America

Part of the conservation involved botanist-led workshops to educate people about how to consider bees when planning their lawns and gardens. The city learned how to support biodiversity in developed areas. As a result, Oslo is a model for other cities to create corridors for bees and other insects. Not only does this bee highway protect insects, it also supports plants and flowers that are at risk.

In 2019, Oslo earned the title of Europe's "Green Capital" for its efforts to support biodiversity in the area.

OVER AND UNDER

Habitat reconnection cannot always involve linked natural spaces. What happens to spotted salamanders that live most of the year in woodland areas but must cross a busy road to reach the **vernal pools** where they mate? Being spotted salamanders, they don't understand the dangers of vehicles on roads. They forge ahead. Some make it. Others do not.

The Wallis Annenberg Wildlife Crossing over the 10 lanes of Highway 101 in California is the largest in the world. Take a look at a time lapse video of its construction. Are there any drawbacks to this wildlife crossing?

🔎 Wallis Annenberg Crossing video

PS

This is the reality for a lot of wildlife, resulting in millions of animal deaths every year. What's the solution? Getting rid of roads isn't practical. But what about wildlife passages that go over and under roads?

In Virginia, the Center for Urban Habitats identified a place where those spotted salamanders needed to cross a busy road. Scientists determined that tunnels would help and figured out how many were needed and how big and far apart they should be. They came up with a plan that included a barrier alongside the road to funnel the salamanders and other wildlife toward a tunnel. The salamanders had safe passage!

CONSERVATION SUCCESS

Sometimes, the solution to safe passage is not under the road, but over it. Wildlife bridges are like other bridges, except they are for animals, not cars or trucks. These bridges span roads, even superhighways, to connect habitats. The bridges are covered with dirt and natural vegetation to mimic natural habitats. Often, people install fences along the roadway to make wildlife use the bridges instead of trying to cross in front of vehicles.

A team of engineers, wildlife biologists, governments, transportation departments, and others get involved in building wildlife bridges. The idea for wildlife bridges originated in France during the 1950s. These bridges have existed in Europe for decades. In North America, beginning in 1996, Canada built a series of corridors over and under the Trans-Canada Highway in Banff National Park. Six of the corridors are bridges. Once the corridors were completed, collisions with wildlife fell 80 percent. Studies around the world show a similar reduction in animal deaths where wildlife tunnels or bridges are present. It's safer for humans, too!

A tiger salamander crosses the road in Wisconsin.

RECONNECTING WATERWAYS

Land animals are not the only ones in need of corridors! Dams, roads, **culverts**, and other development have changed the hydrology of ecosystems and created barriers for fish.

Many fish migrate upriver or downriver during different stages of their life to find food, search for warmer or cooler water, avoid predators, and reproduce. This migration is vital to their survival—when they can't migrate, some species decline.

One solution to allow fish to get around a barrier is to give them a ladder. Yes, a ladder for fish! Of course, it is not like a regular ladder. Instead, a fish ladder is a series of pools, each one higher than the next. Fish can jump from one pool to the next, rest, and then repeat the process to detour around an obstacle.

Before under-road tunnels were created for the spotted salamander in Amherst, Massachusetts, volunteers helped salamanders across the road every year. During mating season, people stopped traffic and carried buckets of salamanders across the road.

Another solution to restore passageways for fish can involve dam removal. For example, the Penobscot was once a free-flowing river in what is now the northeastern United States. Millions of fish such as the American eel, the Atlantic salmon, and many other species migrated from the sea to spawn upstream. The river and fish were central to Native culture for thousands of years. Then, European settlers constructed dams and other buildings during the 1800s. Because the route the fish had always taken was blocked, the fish population plummeted. The loss of fish affected not only the Penobscot Nation but also the entire food web, including birds and animals such as eagles, osprey, and otters.

To save and restore the river, during the early 2000s, Penobscot Nation leaders created an alliance with conservation groups, state and federal governments, and scientists. They had a bold idea—purchase two of the dams and then remove them.

After many years of fundraising and gaining public support, they removed the first dam in 2012 and the second in 2013. In other places along the river, groups created natural fishways around dams. These efforts reopened 2,000 miles of river to migrating fish.

In just a few years, the fish migrating upstream numbered into the millions from nearly zero. Fish reached their historic spawning grounds for the first time in more than a century. Not only did the conservation efforts restore natural fish migrations, they also restored a vital part of the Penobscot Nation culture and connection to the river members use for canoeing, fishing, and swimming.

When culverts are replaced, people benefit as well as the fish. Wider culverts and higher bridges mean reduced flooding on roadways during storms.

As with dams, early engineers did not consider fish when they installed culverts under roads and railroad tracks beginning in the 1800s. Although these pipes allow water to flow freely, they are not always fish friendly. Many culverts block migrating fish. In some places, the width of the culvert is much narrower than the natural stream. When that happens, the water moves through the culvert like water through a firehose. Fish migrating upstream are blasted backward.

Excavators begin the breaching of Veazie Dam, part of the Penobscot River Restoration Project.

The problem that culverts created for fish went unnoticed until the mid-1900s, when scientists in the Pacific Northwest reported on disconnected fish habitats. Unlike removing dams, though, replacing old culverts is not complicated. The new culverts only need to be wider and fish friendly!

In 2022, the U.S. Federal Highway Administration started a program to fund the removal of culverts identified as a barrier for migrating fish. Money to replace culverts went to different tribal, local, and state governments and benefitted many species of migrating fish in the United States.

We've seen examples of how different organizations work together to come up with conservation solutions. In the next chapter, we'll learn more ways communities benefit from and take part in conservation.

Young Conservationist: Jack Dalton (United States)

Jack Dalton (2011–) is known as the kid conservationist. At the age of eight, he learned about the habitat destruction affecting his favorite animal—the orangutan. He combined his love of animals and passion for video editing to create fun, educational YouTube videos. To make a video, Dalton interviews experts, conducts research, and writes the script. He even stars in the videos!

Dalton's hope is to educate people and spread awareness about the problems facing wildlife. In addition to making videos, he gives presentations at zoos, schools, and museums and emcees at fundraisers. His work is recognized locally and globally.

Check out Jack Dalton's videos about conservation. How are his videos capturing people's attention and raising awareness?

🔍 Kid Conservationist videos

CREATE A
HABITAT BOARD GAME

IDEAS FOR SUPPLIES

- science journal
- notecards
- large posterboard
- colored pencils or markers
- ruler
- objects to serve as game pieces
- dice

As you've read, habitat fragmentation and loss have a huge impact on wildlife. Using what you learned about fragmentation and habitat reconnection, create a board game that highlights the challenges that wildlife face and the efforts of conservationists to reconnect habitats.

> **Decide what kind of board game you want to create.** Think about your favorite games. Maybe even play a couple of different games to help you decide.

> **Brainstorm and list both the ways that habitat fragmentation and loss affect wildlife and the ways that conservationists are working to reconnect those habitats.** These should be part of the game and will help you define a storyline for the game.

> **List the rules for your game.** What is the goal of the game? How many players can play at a time? How will a player advance? How might a player be helped forward or pushed backward?

> **Select a layout for the game and draw a sketch.** Adjust your sketch as needed.

> **Create the game on the posterboard.** Write out game cards on notecards if your game uses them.

> **Gather friends and family to play the game!** Take notes about what works well and what needs to change. Keep track of questions about the game that come up as you play.

Try This!

Revamp your game based on the notes you took when you played it. Make improvements and adjustments. Consider adding more elements or more game cards. Can you make the game more complex? Can you convey more information about habitat fragmentation and loss to the players? Could the game include more information about efforts around the world to reconnect habitats?

DESIGN A
WILDLIFE CORRIDOR

Wildlife crossings provide safe passages for animals moving between habitats. Time to think like an engineer and a conservationist to design a crossing near you!

IDEAS FOR SUPPLIES

- art supplies (popsicle sticks, hot glue, a tray or shallow pan, cardboard tubes, cardboard, scissors, soil)

❯ **Select an animal or animals in your area.** Consider researching at-risk species in your region.

❯ **Use a map to locate the habitat where your animal lives.** Find a road that intersects this habitat that your animal might have to cross. Determine the best place along this road for a crossing, keeping in mind the needs of both animals and people.

❯ **Consider what type of crossing would best connect the two wildlife habitats.** A tunnel? A bridge? How will the animals be funneled toward the safe crossing? What will this crossing look like?

❯ **Draw a design of your wildlife crossing and indicate how long, tall, and wide the crossing will be.** Provide labels and details.

❯ **What was the most challenging part of designing a corridor?** What other animals might benefit from your corridor?

Try This!

Using your design, build a model of your corridor. How will you encourage animals to take the corridor? If you build a bridge, what should its surface be? Share your model with family and friends. Explain the need for such a structure.

TEXT TO WORLD

Has development where you live made it hard for animals to live there?

Chapter 6

COMMUNITY-BASED
CONSERVATION

Conservation efforts directly affect the people living nearby. Sometimes, those effects are positive—more wildlife and green space, new job opportunities. However, conservation efforts can also affect people's livelihood or culture. Sometimes, it might feel as though outsiders are telling residents what they can do.

Community-based conservation efforts, though, involve people from the local community. Local people can use their voices and even take leadership roles in the effort to protect nature and wildlife.

Local people also often have deep-rooted knowledge of the ecosystem and its wildlife, as well as knowledge of the culture, that outsiders may not know or understand.

A community-based conservation approach respects local knowledge and culture as well as nature. At times, communities initiate and lead local efforts on their own. Other times, they work in partnership with outside scientists, conservation groups, organizations, or governments.

A SHIFT IN PRACTICE

If you had a question or needed help with something, who would you turn to? An expert, right? In conservation, this was not always the case.

For example, in many countries in Africa, outsiders from Western countries have led conservation projects for decades, often without acknowledging or respecting the people who live among the wildlife. Outsiders claimed to know more about the animals than those who lived there. Local people were left out of conversations and decision making about conservation.

How would you feel if someone from another city came to your neighborhood and made lots of changes that affected your daily life without even asking for your opinion?

CONSERVATION SUCCESS

Conservation practices in many parts of Africa are slowly shifting so that local people are at the forefront of the solutions to protect wildlife. Africans are defining conservation for themselves, leading the efforts, and making the decisions.

Kenyan conservation biologist Resson Kantai Duff said in a TedTalk in 2021, "Conservation is about people. I have learned that the people who are keeping lions roaming in Kenya today are warriors and women and children and elders. . . . We will turn back the clock on wildlife declines and really make life better for all of us. It is time for conservation to be broad, broad enough not just to include a species in trouble, but [also] our land and our cultures, our innovation, our story, us."

The roar of an adult male lion can be heard up to five miles away.

In her talk, Duff told the story of a Samburu warrior from Kenya named Jeneria Lekilelei (1989–). As a warrior, it was Lekilelei's job to protect livestock from wildlife, including lions. Lekilelei grew up hating lions and not knowing anything about conservation. He did not understand the importance of lions and saw them only as a threat.

Then, Lekilelei joined the Ewaso Lions team in Kenya, an African-led group that promotes the **coexistence** of people and wildlife. At Ewaso Lions, he learned about the greater ecosystem and conservation. He learned about lions and the benefits of protecting them. For the first time, Lekilelei thought of lions in a positive light. He started educating others and changing people's minds about lions.

Lions are critical to a healthy ecosystem. As the top predator, they keep the populations of herbivores such as zebra and wildebeest healthy and balanced. When species are in balance, their habitats stay healthy, too.

Watch Resson Kantai Duff's TedTalk about community-led conservation efforts in Africa. What does she say about the role of women in conservation??

🔎 Resson Kantai Duff TedTalk

Lekilelei had the skills to track and hunt lions that killed livestock. After his understanding of the value of lions changed, he got an idea. Instead of using his warrior skills to kill the lions, he and other warriors could track the lions and tell everyone where they were. That way, herders could keep their livestock safe and the lions would not be killed. He started the Warrior Watch program, which has saved hundreds of lions.

Ewaso Lions combines its local knowledge with technology. Scientists use GPS collars, remote sensing, and camera traps to track lions' movements. Computer technology helps them collect and analyze information. The combination of tech and community involvement allows the group to patrol more effectively and identify areas that need more focused conservation efforts. As a result of the work of Warrior Watch and Ewaso Lions, the number of lions in the area has tripled.

WORDS TO KNOW

steward: someone who cares for the natural environment responsibly to keep the ecosystem healthy for animals, plants, and the people who live there.

ungulate: a hooved animal.

In the United States, Native people were also left out of conservation efforts for far too long. This is slowly changing. For centuries, Native people were told what to do and how to do it. Governments silenced their voices and left them out of decisions about how to manage natural resources, even though Native tribes had acted as **stewards** of the land and waterways for thousands of years.

Native people are now leading conservation efforts across the country. In the last chapter, you read about the conservation efforts on the Penobscot River. That project was led by the Penobscot Nation. Native people are also leading the effort to restore bison to tribal land where they used to roam free. Across the Great Plains, European settlers killed bison—once numbering in the millions—to near extinction. Bison were an important part of Native culture for thousands of years. Today, Native people are working not only to recover bison populations, but also to reestablish their connection to the animals. As of 2022, 82 tribes managed 20,000 bison.

Beautiful Bison

Bison are burly and shaggy. They might not look like they are doing much as they spend their days grazing and pooping, but they are a keystone species vital to the North American prairie! When they eat the grass, there is more water, light, and nutrients available for other plants to grow. This increases the diversity of plants. The greater plant diversity creates new habitats for insects, birds, and other species.

Not only that, as the massive **ungulates** move, their hooves aerate the soil, allowing water and air into the ground. In addition, bison disperse seeds, which hitch a ride on their fur and fall off in new locations. Bison hooves push seeds into the soil. And bison dung plays an important role in the nutrient cycle on the prairie and is a mini-habitat for microorganism and insect communities!

POACHERS TURNED PROTECTORS

In parts of the world, one of the only ways people can make money or provide food for their families is by poaching wildlife. Often, poachers are unaware that hunting is illegal or that the species they're hunting are endangered. When confronted with the truth, offered incentives, and given training, some poachers become wildlife protectors.

Think back to Chapter 4 and the efforts to recover populations of sea turtles in Florida that are endangered by human development. In other parts of the world, sea turtles are endangered because of poaching. That was the situation for the five species of sea turtles in the Philippines: hawksbill, loggerhead, green, olive ridley, and leatherback. Conservationists started a program to save these turtles and turned to poachers for help.

Watch this TedEd video about the life of sea turtles and how adult turtles beat the odds to grow to full size. Why is the survival rate for sea turtles so low? What can people do to help the species survive more easily?

🔎 TedEd survival sea turtle

CONSERVATION SUCCESS

Poachers already had the skills to find turtle nests. To protect the turtles, conservationists trained locals to tag female turtles so they can be tracked and to carefully collect eggs. The collected eggs are cared for until they hatch.

The new protectors receive four times more money for each egg they collect and hand over to the conservation group than they did from poaching. Plus, people in the community take pride in the work they do to conserve the turtles.

A sea turtle at the Pawikan Conservation Center, where ex-poachers work to save turtle species from being hunted

Credit: Ramon FVelasquez (CC BY-SA 3.0)

In the Philippines, more than 200,000 sea turtle hatchlings have been released into the ocean.

This conservation effort is just one of many that has turned hunters into protectors. Former hunters are now protecting scarlet macaws in Honduras, tigers in India, and rhinos in Namibia, among others!

BATS BELOW THE BRIDGE

In any conservation effort, education is key. In Austin, Texas, education is what saved a colony of 1.5 million Brazilian free-tailed bats.

When the Congress Avenue Bridge was renovated in the early 1980s, the spaces underneath the bridge became perfect **roosting sites** for migrating bats. The nooks were not too big and not too small. They provided a place safe from predators. And the concrete kept the bats warm on cool nights.

But people did not want them there. They thought the bats would attack people, spread disease, harm the bridge, and reduce water quality in the river below. A group of concerned citizens decided the bats must go.

Tech Used to Stop Poaching

Anti-poaching efforts use many different technologies to catch poachers. Drones are one of these technologies. Drones can efficiently monitor a vast territory in real time. Some drones are even fitted with **thermal imaging technology**, making it harder for poachers to hide. In addition, scientists use **artificial intelligence (AI)** to predict poachers' movements, generate maps of high-risk areas, and outline the best possible patrol routes. People can analyze the DNA of poached animals to pinpoint where the animal came from and identify areas in need of increased patrols. **Smart fences** that detect illegal movement, camera traps, GPS collars, and online databases are all technologies that allow wildlife protectors to respond quickly, minimize threats, and catch poachers.

WORDS TO KNOW

guano: bat poop.

grassroots: operating at a local level by ordinary citizens.

Bat conservationist Merlin Tuttle stepped in and taught people that bats don't carry any more diseases than humans or pets. And if left alone, bats will not attack humans. He also explained how bats are great for pest control. In one night, a colony of bats can eat 10 tons of insects! Studies showed that bat **guano** was not harming the river or the bridge. Because Tuttle shared his knowledge of bats with the public, the bats stayed. Now, they are a tourist attraction in Austin and show the power of education.

Of all life forms on Earth, 90 percent are insects. Scientists estimate there may be 10 million different insect species, yet only 1 million have been identified.

CONSERVATION AT HOME

Remember the bee highway in Oslo? That is an example of community-based conservation. Together, local people, businesses, and the government in Oslo created a connected habitat for bees.

Another example of community-based conservation is Homegrown National Park in the United States. It's community-based rewilding! This is a **grassroots** effort calling on individuals across the county to plant native plants to support biodiversity and restore the ecosystem.

The project began in 2020 with the idea that everyone can play a role in planting native plants and removing invasive ones. If Americans replaced manicured lawns with native grasses, trees, and bushes, they could restore habitats that equal the size of some of the country's

Choose a video on the Homegrown National Park website to watch and learn more about native species of plants and animals and the importance of growing this "national park." Why do people need to act now?

🔎 Homegrown National Park videos

national parks. Many small actions add up to big changes! Conservationist and author Doug Tallamy, one of the cofounders of Homegrown National Park, says, "Don't think about the entire planet's problems—you'll get depressed. Instead, focus on the piece of the earth you can influence."

Mr. Trash Wheel

Mr. Trash Wheel is a low-tech, solar- and water-powered trash collecting device that sits at the mouth of the Jones Falls River in Maryland. Its job is to collect trash before that trash hits Baltimore Harbor.

Mr. Trash Wheel was invented by a local environmental scientist who noticed the amount of trash in the harbor and wanted to do something about it. The city installed the trash-collecting device in May 2014. Right away, the public was fascinated by the trash wheel. A set of googly eyes and a name made it into a celebrity. It even has a social media profile! Not only has Mr. Trash Wheel intercepted more than 5 million pounds of trash, it has also inspired the community to be part of the solution to make waterways safer and cleaner.

Check out this video of Mr. Trash Wheel! Why do you think people are more interested in a device when it has human characteristics?

🔎 Mr. Trash Wheel

WORDS TO KNOW

ornamental plant: a plant grown only for its beauty.

coevolve: when two or more species grow and change together through time, influencing each other's development.

arthropod: an invertebrate animal with a skeleton on the outside of its body. It has a segmented body and jointed legs. Insects and spiders are arthropods.

Homegrown National Park is a science-based approach to increasing biodiversity by creating natural habitats and returning native species to urban and suburban areas. This project helps insects and birds, which in turn support other wildlife.

Many of the invasive species and **ornamental** plants grown in cities and neighborhoods do not support native insects, which have **coevolved** with certain species of native plants. And while insects and other **arthropods** do not need humans, humans do need them—they are critical to food webs and biodiversity. We might think we want mosquitoes to disappear forever, but that would cause major problems for some species of bats and birds that rely on them for food!

A native garden in Denver, Colorado

Young Conservationist: Cash Daniels (United States)

At the age of 7, Cash Daniels (2010–) started his own community-based conservation project: He began cleaning up the waterways near where he lived. By 13, he was spending several hours a week pulling trash out of rivers with other young environmentalists. Their work removed more than 2,000 pounds of aluminum cans from the waterways as well as straws, plastic bottles, and other debris.

In 2022, he and a friend, Ella Grace (2011–), cofounded Cleanup Kids. They wanted to inspire more kids to do cleanups where they live. As Daniels said, "Our individual ripple effects of change, when added together, can quickly create a tidal wave!"

Cleanup Kid crew members tried to do a cleanup once a month or more, counting and documenting the trash they find. Data is a valuable tool for conservationists! Governments and organizations use data when deciding which projects to support.

Visit Daniels's website to learn more about his work and watch a short documentary about his conservation efforts! Do you think it is important for youth to be involved in environmental action?

🔍 Cash Daniels

To save water, Washington County in Utah is paying citizens to remove their lawns and replace them with native plants.

Towns and cities in the United States, including Denver, Minneapolis, and San Francisco, all have community-based conservation efforts to reestablish native plants wherever possible, balancing the needs and interests of people. These are now important landscapes that host a high level of biodiversity.

Many community-based conservation efforts include ecotourism, too, which is the focus of the next chapter.

ESSENTIAL QUESTION

Why should local people be part of conservation efforts in their area?

ACT NOW

Within the pages of this book, you have read about conservation efforts large and small—in this chapter, you learned about people taking action locally. In almost every corner of the world, there is a need for conservation, and it starts with people identifying a problem and then taking action. If you want to conserve plants and animals near you, become a kid conservationist!

❯ Identify an environmental issue near you. Perhaps it's trash along a waterway or a lack of green space or no recycling program at your school. Talk to your friends and family to brainstorm ideas or visit a local park to talk to a ranger.

❯ Design a project. Projects come in all sizes. Yours might be a one-day event to plant native flowers or it could be ongoing trash cleanups once a month. You decide!

❯ Write down what your project will accomplish, why it is needed, how it will get done, and who will be involved. Draw sketches if appropriate.

❯ Enlist the help of friends and family. The more people who know about your project the better— you are raising awareness of an issue.

❯ Brainstorm supplies you will need and start collecting them.

❯ Ask for permission. No matter where your project takes place—whether it is in your yard, at your school, or in a park—you need to ask for permission from the landowner ahead of time. Talk to an adult in charge and describe what you want to do.

❯ Set a date.

❯ Publicize! You need to get the attention and helping hands of even more people in the community.

❯ Act!

Try This!

How did the project go? What went well? What might you do differently next time? Think about how you might expand your project, or create a new one, to involve more community members and increase your impact.

TEXT TO **WORLD**

How do people contribute to conservation where you live? Are there any groups you're interested in joining?

WELCOME
THE BEES

Like all species, bees need shelter, food, and water. Yet all those things are harder to come by in developed areas. So, help a bee out! Although many bee species live in hives, some solitary bee species nest in above-ground holes. That's where you come in. Build a bee hotel to support the solitary, hole-nesting bees in your area. Spring is the best time to make a bee hotel, but you can build one any time of year—you just might have to wait a little longer for visitors.

❯ **Measure the height of the can.** If you are using paper straws or natural stalks, cut them so they are slightly shorter than the can. If you are using sheets of paper, use a pencil to roll them into straw-like tubes, use tape to secure them, and cut the tubes so they are slightly shorter than the can.

❯ **Fill the can with your paper straws, stalks, or tubes.** Your hotel is complete!

❯ **Find a suitable location outdoors for your bee hotel.**
The hotel should be:

* in a sheltered area out of the wind and rain

* firmly attached to something—not dangling or swinging by a string

* between 4 and 7 feet off the ground

* close to native flowering plants

* in a sunny location

❯ **The bee hotel needs room service every year.**
Room service involves cleaning out the bee hotel and replacing the tubes in early summer, after the eggs hatch and the bees check out.

Try This!

The best hotels are those with free breakfast! Provide food for the bees near the hotel. Research native plants in your area and find out which flowers are preferred by solitary, hole-nesting bees. Plant these flowers in several pots. You can start seeds indoors in late winter so they are ready for the bees in the spring. Place the flowers near the hotel.

Chapter 7

ENCOURAGING
ECOTOURISM

Another boost for conservation comes from an unlikely source—tourism. It might not seem logical to try to conserve an ecosystem by inviting tourists. But, if done correctly, ecotourism benefits the visitors, the environment, and the local community.

Ecotourism is responsible travel that minimizes the impact of tourists on both the environment and local culture. For tourists, ecotourism means traveling sustainably while enjoying nature and seeing wildlife.

ESSENTIAL QUESTION

How does tourism play a role in conservation?

Education is a key feature of ecotourism. Visitors learn about the environment and conservation efforts and why an area needs protection. They also engage with the local culture and gain respect for customs by eating delicious food and shopping at local businesses.

Ecotourism creates jobs and economic growth within communities. Ideally, local people are involved in all the decisions around ecotourism so that cultural traditions and values don't get left behind. Locals know the ecosystem and the culture. They often know how to best protect biodiversity, minimize human impact on the environment, and conserve an ecosystem.

Ecotourism takes many different forms. When people travel, you might take a guided tour to view wildlife by foot, vehicle, or boat. For example, visitors might go on a boat ride to see a mangrove forest, walk through a rainforest, or take a safari in a national park in South Africa or Tanzania.

In other places, the government limits the number of visitors. In Manuel Antonio National Park in Costa Rica, the number of visitors is limited to 1,200 per day. This helps reduce the negative impacts large groups of people can have on an ecologically delicate place.

WORDS TO KNOW

hydropower: energy generated by moving water.

renewable energy: power that comes from sources that will never run out, such as the sun and wind.

carbon footprint: the amount of carbon dioxide that is emitted because of someone's daily activities and travel.

emission: something that is released or given off, such as smoke, gas, heat, or light.

compost: to recycle food scraps and vegetation and put them back in the soil.

biodegradable: able to decay and break down.

Tech in Tourism

Technology plays a greater and greater role in our lives—including sustainable tourism. Many hotels and resorts use renewable energy such as sun, wind, and **hydropower**. Staying in hotels that use **renewable energy** lowers visitors' **carbon footprints**. Bicycle-sharing programs and electric vehicles lower carbon **emissions**, too. Innovations in recycling, **composting**, and **biodegradable** products reduce waste in tourist destinations. And water-saving technologies used in ecotourism include water recycling and low-flow fixtures.

As countries develop opportunities for ecotourism, many turn to sustainable building practices. Environmentally friendly building materials, natural light, green roofs, and native landscaping all lower the environmental impact of visitors.

CONSERVATION SUCCESS

Sometimes, travelers take part in conservation volunteer work such as patrolling beaches for turtle nests, planting trees, or collecting data on endangered species. Visitors might also choose to stay in eco-friendly lodging. These are hotels or resorts that are committed to reducing their carbon footprint through recycling, reducing waste, installing energy-efficient lights and appliances, and using renewable energy such as solar or wind. And ecotourism often brings in scientists to study ecosystems and wildlife and gather information.

INDIA'S FIRST GREEN VILLAGE

The Khonoma Nature Conservation and Tragopan Sanctuary is home to nearly 200 bird species as well as more than 70 mammal species.

For the Angami people of Khonoma in northeast India, hunting was part of their cultural tradition. But with the increased use of guns, wildlife became overhunted and more and more difficult to find. During the 1990s, the village elders sensed disaster. To protect their future and connection to the natural world, the Angami knew they needed to protect the animals.

In 1998, the Khonoma Nature Conservation and Tragopan Sanctuary (KNCTS) was established, along with a ban on hunting and logging. It was the first community-based conservation project in India.

A Eurasian tree sparrow in Khonoma

Credit: Dibyendu Ash (CC BY-SA 4.0)

The village council invited conservation experts to the village to offer educational workshops for locals. People who once hunted were paid to protect the forests. And the village encouraged ecotourism to generate income.

> **Visit the Galapagos Conservancy website to learn about the variety of ongoing conservation efforts on the islands.** What conservation approaches does this organization use?
>
> 🔎 Galapagos Conservancy

Some locals did not like the end of the hunting tradition. But word about India's "Green Village" spread, and ecotourists, birders, and researchers began to visit. Each visitor must pay a registration fee, which supports the forest patrols and village development.

Khonoma is more **self-sufficient** than it used to be and it no longer relies on forest resources.

Young Conservationists: Vihaan and Nav Agarwal (India)

Vihaan and Nav Agarwal launched their youth organization, One Step Greener, in 2018 when they were ages 14 and 11. The brothers witnessed firsthand the problem of waste and how the burning of waste in landfills contributes to air pollution in Delhi, India. To address the issue, they started collecting and separating waste from 15 homes to keep it out of the landfill. That number grew to more than 25,000 homes, businesses, and schools.

One Step Greener focuses on the management of waste and promotes recycling and the planting of trees. It also works to educate people about how to responsibly sort and dispose of waste. The long-term goal is sustainability and a zero-waste India.

> **Learn more about One Step Greener and the work it does on its website. Can you think of ways to help your community as the Agarwal brothers have done?**
>
> 🔎 One Step Greener

CONSERVATION SUCCESS

THE GALAPAGOS

The Galapagos Islands, 600 miles off the coast of Ecuador in the Pacific Ocean, are known for their biodiversity. The first tourists visited there by cruise ship in 1934 and the number of visitors has been on the rise ever since. People go to see the stunning scenery and unique wildlife, much of which is found only on the islands. Galapagos sea lions, Darwin's finches, Galapagos hawks, and Galapagos penguins are some of the rare species found there.

Ecotourism brings in money, creates job opportunities for local communities, and supports ongoing conservation efforts. People want to visit Galapagos Islands because of their richly diverse wildlife, and this prompts locals and governments to do even more to protect that wildlife.

Many species of plants and wildlife are endemic to the Galapagos Islands, including 97 percent of its mammals and reptiles and 80 percent of its birds.

Galapagos marine iguanas sunning themselves on Santiago Island

However, ecotourism can be complicated. More people mean more pollution, more strain on local resources, and more chances for invasive species to enter the ecosystem.

In the Galapagos, boat tours are regulated to prevent too many people in one location at the same time. Strict rules and regulations control where visitors can go. Tour providers must minimize their energy and water use, consume local products, and employ local people.

The small country of Costa Rica has more than 25 national parks, 58 wildlife refuges, and dozens of other forest reserves, protected zones, wetland areas, and biological reserves.

Tours provide visitors a chance to swim, snorkel, hike, and visit reserves. Visitors also learn about the biodiversity on the islands and the need to protect it and about the importance of traveling sustainably.

Travel Responsibly

Everyone can be an ecotourist, whether they travel to nearby wilderness parks or to locations far from home. Start by doing research ahead of time. Visit websites to get a better understanding of the steps taken to conserve natural resources and protect ecosystems as well as to support local communities.

› Turn off lights, take short showers, and reuse towels.

› Carry reusable straws and utensils, shopping bags, and food containers.

› Use local public transportation.

› Be aware of local regulations.

› Learn about the ecosystem and ongoing conservation efforts.

› Learn about the local culture and be respectful of customs and traditions.

› Eat, shop, and stay at local businesses.

› Take tours guided by locals.

› Visit places known for their conservation efforts.

› Stay in eco-friendly lodging.

ECOTOURISM AROUND THE WORLD

A gray whale at San Ignacio Lagoon

Credit: ryan harvey (CC BY 2.0)

San Ignacio Lagoon

San Ignacio Lagoon in Mexico is a gray whale nursery. When the whales migrate back to the lagoon from Alaska, fishing is banned. Locals who make their living from fishing turn to ecotourism and provide lodging and tours for visitors. Locals also patrol the area to ensure the whales are not harmed or harassed and that people are not fishing illegally.

Ecotourism lodging is often very different from traditional hotels—visitors might sleep in a yurt, beachside cabana, or even a treehouse!

Tongariro National Park

Credit: Krzysztof Golik (CC BY-SA 4.0)

Tongariro National Park

In New Zealand, ecotourism benefits ecosystems, cultural heritage, the local economy, and visitors. Tongariro National Park, one New Zealand's many national parks, was established in 1887 and has three active volcanoes as well as lakes, waterfalls, and hot springs. It is an important cultural and spiritual site of the Native Māori, who help manage the park to preserve the landscape and their values.

A firefly

Great Smoky Mountains National Park

The animals that draw the greatest crowds to Great Smoky Mountains National Park in the eastern United States are synchronous fireflies that perform for two weeks every June. They emerge at dusk and blink together in a pulsating, rhythmic pattern that is part of their mating ritual. To protect the fireflies and their habitat, the park issues only a limited number of passes each night.

A rainforest in Costa Rica

Credit: eflon

Costa Rica

Costa Rica is a model for ecotourism. Tourists can walk across bridges suspended in the rainforest canopy to spot animals such as toucans, sloths, and howler monkeys. They can also visit the Atlantic and Pacific coasts, climb volcanoes, and observe the nesting sites of green sea turtles. More than 90 percent of the country's energy is renewable, and more than 25 percent of its land is protected.

Tanzania

Tanzania offers a variety of ecotourism activities and more than 30 percent of its land area is protected. Tourists can visit Gombe National Park to see chimpanzees in a supported habitat. Walking safaris in Ngorongoro Conservation area support the Maasai community. Mount Kilimanjaro and the Serengeti are other highlights. Ecotourism in Africa provides hundreds of thousands of jobs.

Chimps in Gombe National Park

Credit: Cethuyghe (CC BY-SA 4.0)

Young Conservationists: Amy and Ella Meek (United Kingdom)

Travelers to a pristine natural landscape don't want to see any plastic pollution, right? The Kids Against Plastic (KAP) organization was founded in 2016 by environmentalist sisters Amy and Ella Meek, who were 12 and 10 at the time. Both are passionate about tackling the problem of plastic pollution. They founded KAP to educate youth about environmental issues and empower them to act.

KAP has resources on its website for kids and schools about ways they can help and campaigns to join. One in a Million is a challenge with the goal to pick up one million pieces of litter. In addition, KAP has a club of like-minded youth who want to learn about environmental issues and be leaders of change.

Amy and Ella have worked with more than 1,800 schools and businesses. They also raise awareness of plastic pollution by speaking at TEDx conferences and even to governments as well as at the United Nations youth summit.

Ecotourism benefits communities, the ecosystem, and travelers! Another type of conservation effort involves laws and protections, which you will read about next.

ESSENTIAL QUESTION

How does tourism play a role in conservation?

TEXT TO **WORLD**

If you could visit one natural area on Earth, where would it be? Why?

CREATE AN
ECOTOURISM TRAVEL BROCHURE

Ecotourism can have benefits for travelers, local communities, and ecosystems. Spread the word about ecotourism with a brochure!

❯ **Choose a location you would like to promote.** It could be a local place, an area you would like to visit, or a place that interests you.

❯ **Research the ecotourism opportunities as well as reasons people should visit.** Investigate possible activities such as tours, cultural experiences, recreation, lodging, and restaurants.

Check out this website and infographic to learn more about the different types of ecotourism. Which type of ecotourism would you most like to participate in?

🔎 Homegrown National Park videos

❯ **Find out about the wildlife and ecosystems.** Are there any conservation efforts in that area?

❯ **Research the local culture.** What are the customs, traditions, and food?

❯ **To make the brochure, lay the paper horizontally and fold into equal thirds.** You should have six panels, three on the front and three on the back. Close the brochure to locate the front cover panel.

❯ **On the front cover, draw an image of the ecotourism destination and include a title.**

❯ **Plan where the rest of the information you collected will go inside the brochure.** Place the information on the panels and include drawings, headings, and subheadings. Choose extra details you want to add, such as a packing list, best time of year to travel, how much time to spend there, sample itineraries, cost, or a map.

❯ **Share your brochure with friends, classmates, and family to explain the benefits of ecotourism.**

Try This!

Spread the word further. Using your research, create a podcast or video advertisement. Perhaps plan to put several posts on social media to help spread the word.

DESIGN A
SCAVENGER HUNT

IDEAS FOR SUPPLIES

- science journal
- pencil

Whenever you visit a wild place, slowing down to look and listen is an important part of the experience. Scavenger hunts can help you do that. Design one for your next trip, but make it about seeing, hearing, and smelling, not about collecting items.

❯ **Research the place you plan to visit, whether it is a local park or wilderness area or one farther away.**

❯ **Visit the official website as well as find sources such as videos.** What are you likely to see, hear, and smell in that location?

❯ **Decide whether you want your scavenger hunt to be about noticing specific things (such as certain species of birds) or if you want it to be more general—or both!**

❯ **Consider whether you want your scavenger hunt to have a theme—it can, but it doesn't have to.** Possible ideas include finding opposites (large/small, smooth/rough) or colors, identifying certain species, or finding items beginning with certain letters of the alphabet.

❯ **List items for your scavenger hunt.** Remember, each item on the list can be specific, general, or a mix. Consider adding items you might hear and smell, not just see, in that location.

❯ **Decide if you want to have the scavenger hunters photograph, draw, or video the items to log what they find.**

❯ **Finalize the list and the instructions.** Go!

Try This!

If you have friends or extended family that may visit the area, share your scavenger hunt with them. When you and others visit this area, consider taking a trash bag and gloves to collect bits of trash you find. Do your part to help the areas you visit!

Chapter 8

LAWS AND
PROTECTIONS

Anytime we visit a park, sanctuary, marine park, or wilderness area of any size, we witness conservation in action. Look around—everything there, from the land and water to the animals and plants, is protected and carefully managed.

Many protected areas have rules that visitors must follow. Those rules might include the need to stay on the trails, pack out all trash, not fly drones, and not harass or approach wildlife. In some places, hunting or fishing with a permit might be legal at certain times of the year, while in other places it might be completely illegal. Sometimes, areas are temporarily closed to visitors, perhaps because it's nesting season for birds or an area has been overused and needs to rest and regenerate. Usually, picking flowers or take any natural resources such as rocks is forbidden.

ESSENTIAL QUESTION

How do laws help with conservation around the world?

CONSERVATION SUCCESS

These rules and regulations are good things! They allow people to enjoy nature now and protect it for the future—that's conservation at work.

THE FIRST LAWS

One of the first conservation laws in the United States was the Lacey Act in 1900. The act protects wildlife and plants from illegal poaching and trade. In 1913, the federal government passed the Migratory Bird Act to save declining bird populations—more than 1,000 birds were listed as of 2023.

In the mid-1900s the conservation movement gained strength, and the government passed more laws. They include the Land and Water Conservation Fund Act (1964), the National Wildlife Refuge System Act (1966), the Clean Air Act (1970), and the Clean Water Act (1972).

Laws play a role in conservation, too, from creating protected areas to safeguarding wildlife, land, air, water, and natural resources.

CITES

Some conservation laws are international agreements. The Convention on International Trade in Endangered Species of Wild Fauna and Flora (CITES) was signed in 1973. This treaty with the complicated name has a simple purpose: to protect plants and animals from going extinct because of international trade. In certain cases, the demand for a species is so high that, when combined with other problems such as habitat loss, its survival is threatened. CITES protects these species.

So, do politicians show up to work one day to write and pass a new law? No! Passing laws takes time, and usually everyday people are the ones who first see the need for environmental and conservation laws. These people organize protests, write letters, and raise awareness of problems.

Rachel Carson (1907–1964) was an American biologist, conservationist, and author. She was among the first to recognize the danger of unregulated pesticide use. Many pesticides, including one called DDT, killed not only insects but wildlife, too. After extensive scientific research, she published a book called *Silent Spring* in 1962.

Her readers were astounded at her descriptions of the devastating impacts of DDT on the environment. She wrote, "Can anyone believe it is possible to lay down such a barrage of poison on the surface of the earth without making it unfit for all life? They should not be called 'insecticides' but **'biocides.'**"

Rachel Carson and wildlife artist Bob Hines conducting marine biology research in Florida in 1952.

Chemical companies were angry about the book. They tried to disprove Carson's work, but her research was so thorough it stood up time and again to attack and inspection. In 1972, 10 years after the publication of *Silent Spring*, a federal law to ban DDT was passed—a direct result of Carson's work.

THE ENDANGERED SPECIES ACT

In 1973, the ESA became law. This is one of the most significant conservation laws in the United States. It works to protect threatened and endangered species and recover declining populations.

The ESA makes it illegal to kill, harm, harass, and trap any species on the endangered species list, which is continually updated. The law also requires steps be taken to identify and conserve the habitats where those species live. The ongoing work to recover species and conserve habitats is a partnership among governments at the tribal, local, state, and federal level. The work also involves scientists, conservationists, and private citizens. The ESA has saved many species in the United States from extinction. Here are a few examples.

A bald eagle
Credit: Andy Morffew (CC BY 2.0)

Bald eagle

The bird and national symbol almost went extinct in the mid-1900s due to DDT poisoning. Habitat conservation and the banning of DDT led to the bird's recovery, and it was removed from the list in 2007, 35 years after DDT was banned.

American alligator

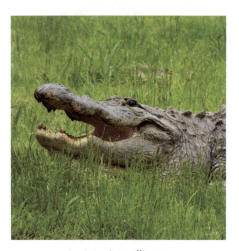

An American alligator
Credit: gailhampshire (CC BY 2.0)

The American alligator, native to the southeastern United States, was an endangered species by the 1960s due to overhunting and habitat loss. Protection under the ESA led to the recovery of the alligator population, and it was delisted in 1987.

Whooping crane

By 1941, only 21 whooping cranes were left because of habitat loss and hunting. Under the ESA, the birds were managed and reintroduced into their native habitat. At the 50th anniversary of the ESA in 2023, more than 500 whooping cranes were in the wild.

A whooping crane

Credit: Mike's Birds (CC BY-SA 2.0)

Read more about the history of the ESA, how it works, and the animals it has protected. What were the key events that led to the ESA?

🔍 NatGeo Kids ESA

West Virginia northern flying squirrel

This unique squirrel species was listed as endangered in 1985 due to habitat loss. By 2013, the squirrel was delisted because of the restoration of its unique, high-elevation hardwood forest and the increase in its population.

A flying squirrel

Tennessee purple coneflower

In 1979, this species of flower was the second plant added to the ESA due to extreme habitat loss in its small range around Nashville, Tennessee. A conservation plan protected its habitat and boosted the population enough that it was removed from the ESA in 2011.

Tennessee coneflowers

Credit: Funke (CC BY-SA 4.0)

WORDS TO KNOW

microplastic: an extremely small piece of plastic that makes its way into the environment and is ingested by wildlife.

BEYOND THE ESA

Conservation laws address many different problems around the world. In 2021, the European Union (EU) banned many types of single-use plastic such as straws and utensils. Then, in 2023, the EU banned the use of **microplastics** in products. These tiny particles are added to many personal hygiene products and glitter, and they never decompose. The plastics eventually make it into the environment and are ingested by wildlife—and people.

Specific laws often protect individual species. The Shark Finning Prohibition Act (2000) and the Shark Conservation Act (2010) protect sharks in the United States. Mountain gorillas in Africa receive protection from many sources, including the Gorilla Agreement,

The Kapiti Island Nature Reserve in New Zealand is run by the country's department of conservation and allows only 160 visitors per day.

which requires each of the 10 countries where the gorillas live to protect the species and its habitat. The conservation efforts improved the gorillas' status from critically endangered to endangered in 2020.

In addition, laws create government agencies to oversee the protection of ecosystems and wildlife. In the United States, they include the NPS, USFWS, and NOAA.

Local governments have similar agencies. Many wildlife refuges, sanctuaries, wilderness areas, national parks, and marine protected areas are created and managed by tribal, state, local, and federal governments.

PROTECTED LAND

American environmentalist and author Wallace Stegner (1909–1993) said in 1983, "National parks are the best idea we ever had."

Humans have set aside and protected certain lands for thousands of years for spiritual and recreational purposes. In the eighteenth century, the Qing Dynasty in Mongolia established the Bogd Khan Uul as a protected site. Some consider this to be the world's first protected area. In March of 1872, Yellowstone National Park was established, becoming the world's first national part. Now, more than 4,000 national parks exist around the world, including more than 400 in the United States. Parks protect diverse habitats, from mountains to deserts to rainforests to tundra, wetlands, and more.

Bogd Khan Mountain in Mongolia, part of an area protected since 1783

Protected lands may be managed by tribal, state, or local governments, or even by organizations or private individuals. For example, in 1938, Rosalie Edge established the Hawk Mountain Sanctuary in Pennsylvania to protect birds of prey. Originally 1,400 acres, the **nonprofit** sanctuary now covers 2,600 acres that not only provides refuge for birds but also serves as a hub for scientific research and public education.

Young Conservationist: Xiye Bastida (Mexico & United States)

Xiye Bastida (2002–) grew up in San Pedro Tultepec near Mexico City, Mexico, as part of the Otomi-Toltec Indigenous community. She was raised believing in the philosophy "of taking care of Mother Earth because Mother Earth takes care of us."

As a teen, she and her family moved to New York, where she began her journey as a climate justice activist and joined the ongoing climate movement. Bastida organized climate strikes both at her school and citywide. She spoke publicly about climate justice, Indigenous rights, and the intersection of the two. Bastida wants youth and communities most affected by climate change to be involved in the climate movement and in decision making. And she wants Indigenous knowledge to be part of the solution for the climate crisis.

MARINE PROTECTED AREAS

Not all protected areas are on land! Marine protected areas (MPAs) are the protected wilderness areas of the sea. Many MPAs conserve marine ecosystems and natural resources. Other MPAs protect cultural or historic sites such as shipwrecks, lighthouses, submerged ancient coastal settlements, and Indigenous fishing and cultural sites.

MPAs protect a variety of habitats, including coasts, coral reefs, mangrove swamps, **estuaries**, and open ocean. The United States has close to 1,000 MPAs, which protect 26 percent of U.S. waters. Among them are the Papahānaumokuākea Marine National Monument of Hawaii, the Florida Keys, and even freshwater habitats in the Great Lakes region.

MPAs all around the world protect marine ecosystems and recover populations of marine species. Raja Ampat near West Papua, Indonesia, is a network of MPAs. The first one was established in 2004, and Raja Ampat now spans thousands of square miles of ocean and more than 1,400 islands. The region is full of biodiversity. One species in particular, the reef manta ray, needed protection.

Overhunting in the area threatened the reef manta ray. The creation of the MPA, which included a ban on hunting, helped the population recover. Not only that, but a combination of community-based conservation and ecotourism played a huge role in the effort.

> **Watch the Smithsonian's video on MPAs in the United States.** How are MPAs like an insurance policy?
>
> ꡒ Smithsonian marine protected areas

Studies to track manta rays utilize photo identification. Each manta ray has a unique pattern of spots, just like humans have unique fingerprints. Using the identification database, researchers found that in one area of the MPA, the number of rays more than doubled, from 210 to 511 rays. The studies show that even though reef manta ray populations continue to decline in other parts of the world, the conservation efforts in Raja Ampat are working.

The success in Raja Ampat can help with planning future MPA conservation and to educate governments, scientists, businesses, organization, and everyday people.

Throughout this book you have read about protected areas and conservation efforts of all types and sizes. Think back to the privately owned 3,500-acre Knepp Estate in England and Mozambique's Gorongosa National Park, which covers more than 1,500 square miles. You learned about the restoration at Cuyahoga Valley National Park and how the Zasavica Special Nature Reserve in Serbia was the perfect place to reintroduce Eurasian beavers. And there is the Terai Arc Landscape in Asia that connects habitats, the Khonoma Nature Conservation and Tragopan Sanctuary in India started by the community, and protected spaces in Oslo that create a bee highway. Each one of these protected spaces heals ecosystems and supports biodiversity.

What actions will you take to protect ecosystems and biodiversity? You can start by sharing what you know! When you share your knowledge, more people will understand the need for continued conservation and the ways all individuals can make a difference.

ESSENTIAL QUESTION

How do laws help with conservation around the world?

TEST
YOUR TRASH

Have you ever thought about what happens to your trash when you throw it away? Scientists and environmentalists have! Many of the environmental laws in place today regulate what can be disposed of in landfills and how to dispose of more hazardous materials to prevent soil, water, and air pollution. Most of your household waste ends up in a landfill. What happens next? This experiment will help you understand the types of items that are biodegradable or not, which can inform your buying choices and how you dispose of items.

> **Cut the top of each of the five jugs so you end up with five "pots."** Have an adult help you with the cutting. Fill each jug with soil and label each from 1 to 5. (NOTE: You can also do this outdoors if you have a space where you can bury trash instead of using the pots.)

> **Select the five trash items you want to test.** Choose items that differ from one another. Bury one item in each pot, taking careful notes about what you are putting in each pot. Record the date. Place the pots outdoors so they are exposed to varying temperatures and precipitation.

> **Make some predictions.** How long will each item take before it begins to break down? Which will break down the fastest?

> **After two months or more, dig up each item.** Note the changes. Were your predictions correct?

> **Which types of trash broke down the most?** Were any pieces the same as when you buried them? Were any pieces of trash unrecognizable?

> **How can your results help you decide what to buy and what to throw away?**

IDEAS FOR SUPPLIES

- 5 empty gallon milk jugs
- heavy-duty scissors
- soil
- trowel
- science journal
- protective gloves
- 5 different items to test, such as an apple core (or other food scrap), biodegradable packing peanuts, a piece of scrap paper or newspaper, a plastic straw or utensil, a piece of Styrofoam, an empty toilet paper roll, a biodegradable takeout container, a pencil, a paper towel

Try This!

Rebury your trash in the same container or location and let the decomposition continue. Check on it every two months. What changes do you notice?

CREATE A
MAP OF PROTECTED AREAS

IDEAS FOR SUPPLIES

- posterboard
- colored pencils or markers

Parks, wilderness areas, and protected areas are all over the world. Some may be near you. Investigate the protected areas in your state!

❯ **Research the protected areas in your state.** These may be large or small and managed at the tribal, federal, state, or local levels. Some will be on land. Some may be in water. Identify 5 to 10 you think are most important to conservation.

Visit the NPS website to see an interactive map of all the parks in the United States. Which national parks would you most like to visit? Why?

🔎 NPS Find a Park

❯ **Draw a map of your state on the posterboard.** Include a title, compass rose, and map key.

❯ **Outline on the map each of the protected areas you want to highlight.** Label each and include information about its importance to conservation.

❯ **Consider including information about the history of the area and how it became protected.** How are animal species protected in the area, how is it managed, and what types of habitats are within the ecosystem? Are there any rules for visitors?

❯ **After you finish the map, share it with friends and family.** Ask people which areas they would like to visit and why.

Try This!

Take a field trip! Decide which area or areas you would most like to visit or which are the closest in your state. Take a trip to the protected area. When you arrive, stop at the visitors' center if there is one. Look at the displays to learn even more information about the area. Talk to rangers and volunteers about the role their park plays in conservation. Then, get outside and see conservation in action.

TEXT TO **WORLD**

What rules does your school have to protect wildlife or ecosystems on school grounds?

acidity: the level of acids in a substance such as water and soil. Examples include vinegar and lemon juice.

acoustic monitoring: the use of sound recordings to collect information about different species.

aerate: to allow air to flow through.

agrarian: relating to farmed land.

algae: a simple organism found in water that is like a plant but without roots, stems, or leaves.

amphibian: a cold-blooded animal, such as a toad, frog, or salamander, that relies on its environment to maintain its body temperature. Amphibians live on land and in the water.

Anthropocene: a geologic time during which humans have had a great impact on Earth's environment and climate.

arthropod: an invertebrate animal with a skeleton on the outside of its body. It has a segmented body and jointed legs. Insects and spiders are arthropods.

artificial intelligence (AI): a computer system that can perform tasks that typically require human intelligence.

atmosphere: a layer of gases around the earth.

biocide: a chemical or substance that destroys or kills certain living things.

biodegradable: able to decay and break down.

biodiversity: the variety of life on Earth.

captive breeding: the process of mating wild species to produce and raise offspring in places such as zoos, aquariums, and other conservation facilities.

carbon footprint: the amount of carbon dioxide that is emitted because of someone's daily activities and travel.

carnivore: an animal that eats meat.

citizen science: the involvement of everyday people in scientific activities or projects.

clear-cutting: to remove every tree from an area.

climate change: the long-term change in temperature and weather patterns across a large area, in particular attributed to the use of fossil fuels as an energy source.

coevolve: when two or more species grow and change together through time, influencing each other's development.

coexistence: living together at the same time or in the same place.

compost: to recycle food scraps and vegetation and put them back in the soil.

conservation: the management and protection of wildlife and natural resources.

crops: plants grown for food and other uses.

culture: the beliefs and way of life of a group of people, which can include religion, language, art, clothing, food, and holidays.

culvert: a pipe made of metal or concrete to move water underneath roads and railroad tracks.

data: facts or pieces of information, often given in the form of numbers, that can be processed by a computer.

decompose: to rot or break down.

deforestation: the act of completely cutting down and clearing trees.

degraded: harmed to the point where an ecosystem does not function properly.

depleted: used up.

disperse: to spread out over a wide area.

drought: a long period of unusually low rainfall that can harm plants and animals.

ecosystem: an interdependent community of living and nonliving things and their environment.

ecosystem engineer: a species that greatly alters an ecosystem by creating, modifying, maintaining, or destroying it.

ecotourism: tourism that responsibly protects wildlife and the environment and supports conservation.

emission: something that is released or given off, such as smoke, gas, heat, or light.

endangered species: at risk of becoming extinct.

Endangered Species Act (ESA): a law in the United States that identifies threatened and endangered species. The listed species are protected and their habitats are conserved.

endemic: native to a particular place.

environment: everything in nature, living and nonliving, including plants, animals, soil, rocks, and water.

eradicate: to eliminate, remove, or destroy something.

erosion: the gradual wearing away of rock or soil by water and wind.

estuary: a partly enclosed coastal body of water that has rivers and streams flowing into it and is connected to the ocean.

extinction: the death of an entire species so that it no longer exists.

feces: poop.

GLOSSARY

flyway: an air route used by migrating birds.

food web: a network of connected food chains that shows the complex set of feeding relationships between plants and animals.

fossil fuel: a fuel such as oil, coal, or natural gas, which takes millions of years to form from the remains of plant and animals.

fragmented: broken or separated.

fungus: a group of plant-like organisms that are neither plants nor animals. They are decomposers that live off dead or decaying matter. Examples include mushrooms, mold, and yeast. Plural is fungi.

gene: a section of DNA that codes for a particular trait. DNA stands for deoxyribonucleic acid, the substance found in cells that carries genes, the genetic information that contains the blueprint of an organism.

genetic diversity: the variety of genes within a species.

geologic timescale: the way time is divided into large blocks to describe the 4.6-billion-year history of the earth.

geologist: a scientist who studies geology, which is the history and structure of the earth and its rocks.

GPS collar: a collar placed on an animal that uses the Global Positioning System to track the animal.

grassroots: operating at a local level by ordinary citizens.

greenhouse gas: a gas in the atmosphere that traps heat. Too much greenhouse gas contributes to global warming.

guano: bat poop.

habitat: a plant's or animal's natural home that supplies it with food, water, and shelter.

habitat island: a small, isolated habitat cut off from other habitats by roads, dams, or urban development.

harmony: in peace and agreement.

hazardous waste: a waste with properties that make it dangerous or potentially harmful to human health or the environment.

herbivore: an animal that eats only plants.

holistic: considering the whole of something, not just its parts.

hydrology: the distribution and movement of water in an ecosystem.

hydropower: energy generated by moving water.

incentive: a reward that encourages someone to do something.

indigenous: native people who originally settled a region; also known as First Nation or First Peoples.

industrialized: having many businesses and factories involved in producing goods.

Industrial Revolution: a period during the eighteenth and nineteenth centuries when large-scale production of goods began and large cities and factories began to replace small towns and farming.

intertidal: the zone where the ocean meets the land between low and high tides.

invasive species: a plant or animal that is not native to an area and may cause it harm.

keystone species: a species that plays a vital role in an ecosystem and without which the ecosystem would be greatly altered.

larva: the wormlike stage of an insect's life. The plural is larvae.

life cycle: the growth and changes a living thing goes through, from birth to death.

livestock: animals raised for food and other uses.

mammal: a type of animal, such as a human, dog, or cat. Mammals are born live, feed milk to their young, and usually have hair or fur covering most of their skin.

marine: having to do with the ocean.

microchip: to fit an animal with a tiny chip under its skin so the animal can be identified.

microorganism: a living organism that is so small you can see it only with a microscope.

microplastic: an extremely small piece of plastic that makes its way into the environment and is ingested by wildlife.

migrate: to move from one environment to another when seasons change.

natural resource: a material or substance such as gold, wood, and water that occurs in nature and is valuable to humans.

nonprofit: an organization that operates for social, environmental, or cultural purposes instead of for making money.

nutrient cycle: how nutrients, the substances in food and soil that living things need to grow and survive, move through an ecosystem.

nutrients: substances in food, water, and soil that living things need to live and grow.

offspring: an animal's young.

organic: something that is or was living, such as animals, wood, grass, and insects. Also refers to food grown naturally, without chemicals.

organism: something living, such as a plant or an animal.

ornamental plant: a plant grown only for its beauty.

over-exploitation: the taking of a natural resource faster than it can reproduce or be replenished. To exploit means to use something for personal gain without respect for the consequences.

pesticide: a chemical used to kill pests such as rodents or insects.

philanthropist: a person who helps others by donating money, time, or property.

photomosaic: a large picture created using many small photos.

poacher: someone who illegally hunts, traps, or kills wildlife.

pollinate: to transfer pollen from the male parts of flowers to the female parts so that flowers can make seeds.

prairie: a vast area of open grassland.

predator: an animal that hunts and eats other animals.

preservationist: a person who believes that nature should be protected from all human use and impact.

prey: an animal hunted and eaten by other animals.

profit: financial or some other gain.

pupate: to turn into a pupa, one stage of an insect's life cycle.

rainforest: a forest in a hot climate that gets a lot of rain every year, so the plants are very green and grow a lot.

reconnecting: the reestablishment of a connection between two habitats.

regenerate: the ability to renew, reestablish, or recover from damage.

rehabilitate: to restore something to its previous condition.

reintroduction: the process of returning a species to an area where it once lived but had been absent from.

reproduce: to make something new, just like itself. To have babies.

reptile: an animal such as a snake, lizard, alligator, or turtle that has a spine, lays eggs, has scales or horny places, and breathes air. Reptiles are cold-blooded, so they need sunlight to keep warm and shade to stay cool.

restoration: the recovery of a damaged or destroyed habitat to its natural state.

revegetate: to replant and rebuild the soil of disturbed land.

rewilding: the restoration of an ecosystem and its biodiversity to minimize human impact and let nature take care of itself.

roosting site: a place where birds and bats go to rest or sleep.

runoff: water that flows off the land into bodies of water. It picks up wastes as it flows over the surface of the ground. Runoff can pollute streams, lakes, rivers, and oceans.

rural: in the countryside, as opposed to a city.

satellite remote sensing: the use of special cameras to monitor an area's physical characteristics from a distance.

secretion: a fluid produced by an organism.

self-sufficient: not needing help from others.

sewage: waste from buildings carried away through sewers.

smart fence: an invisible fence that uses technology to detect movement and provide alerts.

spawn: to produce eggs or young.

species: a group of plants or animals that are closely related and produce offspring.

steward: someone who cares for the natural environment responsibly to keep the ecosystem healthy for animals, plants, and the people who live there.

subtropical: an area close to the tropics where the weather is warm.

sustainability: the use of Earth's resources in a way that keeps the planet healthy now and for the future.

technology: the tools, methods, and systems used to solve a problem or do work.

territorial: relating to the space an animal needs and defends in order to find resources and mates.

thermal imaging technology: a tool that detects and measures heat, creating a thermal image of people or wildlife in the dark.

threatened species: a species that is likely to become endangered in future.

trait: a specific characteristic of an organism determined by genes or the environment.

tropical: the hot climate zone to the north and south of the equator.

ungulate: a hooved animal.

urban: in a city or large town.

vernal pool: a shallow depression in the ground that holds water for part of the year and provides a habitat for animals and plants.

wetland: an area where the land is saturated with water. Wetlands are important habitats for fish, plants, and wildlife.

wildlife: animals, birds, and other living things that live wild in nature.

wildlife corridor: a passageway, either natural or manmade, that connects habitats and allows wildlife to move safely from one to another.

Metric Conversions

Use this chart to find the metric equivalents to the English measurements in this book. If you need to know a half measurement, divide by two. If you need to know twice the measurement, multiply by two. How do you find a quarter measurement? How do you find three times the measurement?

English	Metric
1 inch	2.5 centimeters
1 foot	30.5 centimeters
1 yard	0.9 meter
1 mile	1.6 kilometers
1 pound	0.5 kilogram
1 teaspoon	5 milliliters
1 tablespoon	15 milliliters
1 cup	237 milliliters

ESSENTIAL QUESTIONS

Introduction: Why is conservation so important?

Chapter 1: What strategies do scientists use to restore ecosystems?

Chapter 2: How is rewilding an effective approach to conservation?

Chapter 3: Why is it important to reintroduce species to ecosystems?

Chapter 4: Why is the recovery of an individual species an important part of conservation?

Chapter 5: Why is it important to reconnect wild spaces on land and in the water?

Chapter 6: Why should local people be part of conservation efforts in their area?

Chapter 7: How does tourism play a role in conservation?

Chapter 8: How do laws help with conservation around the world?

BOOKS

French, Jess. *It's a Wonderful World : How to Protect the Planet and Change the Future*. DK Children, 2022.

Latham, Donna. *Backyard Biology: Discover the Life Cycles and Adaptations Outside Your Door with Hands-On Science Activities*. Nomad Press, 2020.

Montgomery, Sy. *Condor Comeback* (Scientists in the Field). Clarion Books, 2020.

Newman, Patricia. *A River's Gifts : The Mighty Elwha River Reborn*. Millbrook Press, 2023.

Paul, Miranda. *101 Ways to Help the Earth with Dr. Seuss's Lorax*. Random House, 2022.

Steen, David A. *Rewilding: Bringing Wildlife Back Where It Belongs*. Neon Squid, 2022.

Stevens, Alison Pearce. *Animal Climate Heroes!* Godwin Books/Henry Holt and Co., 2024.

Tallamy, Douglas W. *Nature's Best Hope: A New Approach to Conservation That Starts in Your Yard* (Young Readers' Edition). Timber Press, 2020.

WEBSITES

Coral Restoration Foundation
coralrestoration.org

Earth Day's 52 Ways to Invest in Our Planet
earthday.org/earth-day-tips

Merlin Tuttle's Bat Conservation
merlintuttle.org

REI's How to Take Climate Action
rei.com/blog/stewardship/how-to-take-climate-action

Smithsonian's National Zoo & Conservation Biology Institute
nationalzoo.si.edu/conservation-ecology-center

The Bee Conservancy
thebeeconservancy.org

RESOURCES

SELECTED BIBLIOGRAPHY

oysterworldwide.com/news/conservation-around-world

environmentalscience.org/conservation

nhpbs.org/wild/environmentalism.asp

amphibianrescue.org/about/history

education.nationalgeographic.org/resource/zoo

nwf.org/our-work/wildlife-conservation/success-stories

nationalgeographic.com/animals

earthday.org/history

nps.gov/articles/000/the-devoted-people-behind-big-data-in-national-parks.htm

aspeninstitute.org/blog-posts/community-science-a-powerful-tool-for-conservation

education.nationalgeographic.org/resource/importance-marine-protected-areas

bbc.com/travel/article/20120426-travelwise-birth-and-spread-of-the-worlds-national-parks

QR CODE GLOSSARY

Page 5: rmpbs.pbslearningmedia.org/resource/ctv21-conservation-biology-video/camp-tv

Page 5: anthropocene.wescreates.wesleyan.edu/anthropocene/the-anthropocene-for-kids-with-podcast

Page 6: licypriyakangujam.com/about

Page 8: birds.cornell.edu/home/citizen-science-be-part-of-something-bigger

Page 11: youtube.com/watch?v=5tRMqbPH_pk

Page 17: pbskids.org/scigirls/citizen-science#:~:text=Citizen%20science%20happens%20when%20ordinary,Anyone%20can%20do%20citizen%20science!

Page 19: theconversation.com/beavers-offer-lessons-about-managing-water-in-a-changing-climate-whether-the-challenge-is-drought-or-floods-168545

Page 21: fisheries.noaa.gov/podcast/restoring-floridas-iconic-coral-reefs

Page 22: vimeo.com/231468290?login=true

Page 25: kansasdiscovery.org/making-a-flipbook-discovery-at-home

Page 27: ed.ted.com/lessons/why-is-biodiversity-so-important-kim-preshoff

Page 31: gorongosa.org/our-gorongosa-film

Page 33: rewildingeurope.com/world-rewilding-day

QR CODE GLOSSARY (CONT.)

Page 35: rewildology.com/category/topics/rewilding

Page 40: iucnredlist.org/about/background-history

Page 41: rootsandshoots.org/for-youth

Page 43: weforum.org/agenda/2022/08/endangered-species-reintroduced-biodiversity

Page 45: butterfly-conservation.org/our-work

Page 47: youtube.com/watch?v=yeXMlAjJUKw

Page 52: instagram.com/amphibianrescue/reel/ChP-k4ADIqY/

Page 53: evaccfoundation.org/index.php/en/home

Page 54: ed.ted.com/lessons/can-zoos-actually-save-species-from-extinction-nigel-rothfels

Page 54: cbsnews.com/news/de-extinction-bringing-animal-species-back-from-the-brink

Page 58: youtube.com/watch?app=desktop&v=AkGnPl0QL6o

Page 61: species-in-pieces.com

Page 63: nps.gov/subjects/invasive/what-are-invasive-species.htm#:~:text=Invasive%20species%20has%20a%20specific,health%20(Executive%20Order%2013751).

Page 66: floridawildlifecorridor.org/maps

Page 67: abcbirds.org/blog/north-american-bird-flyways

Page 69: 101wildlifecrossing.org

Page 73: kidconservationist.com/videos

Page 79: ted.com/talks/resson_kantai_duff_why_africa_needs_community_led_conservation?subtitle=en

Page 81: ed.ted.com/lessons/the-survival-of-the-sea-turtle

Page 85: homegrownnationalpark.org/videos

Page 85: mrtrashwheel.com

Page 87: theconservationkid.com/2024/12/26/trust-your-wild-side

Page 93: galapagos.org/projects

Page 93: onestepgreener.org

Page 99: esgholist.com/ecotourism-an-infographic-introduction

Page 105: kids.nationalgeographic.com/history/article/endangered-species-act

Page 109: ocean.si.edu/conservation/solutions-success-stories/marine-protected-areas

Page 112: nps.gov/findapark/index.htm